JOURNEY TO THE PROMISED LAND

(From Egypt to the Promised Land)

OVERLOOKING THE PROMISED LAND

William Johnston

Contents

Introduction

Numbers 21.8 , John 9.41 , I Corinthians 10.12 are the key verses shared here to introduce the purpose of this book. It is aimed at no particular person but for everyone in the Lord, especially the "wandering" Christian who may have fallen out of the fellowship of the Lord God (I John 1.3). Falling out of the fellowship of the Lord is not the same as losing our own salvation. Once you are saved in the Lord, then you start to backslide. This does not mean you are losing your salvation in the Lord but simply falling out of fellowship with the Lord or the church.

The purpose of this book is to give us some insights and enlightenment into our spiritual journey in comparison to the wilderness experiences of the Hebrew nation from the Egyptian bondage to the Promised Land. Hence, "these things were our examples (I Corinthians 10.11)."

It must be understood first that the atonement of Jesus Christ was necessary (2 Corinthians 5.19). It was both legal and practical, as will be explained later. Redemption on the cross was the only way to shed light on us and on those in the fallen state.

Of all the events taken place in the Genesis account of Adam and Eve and throughout the Biblical history is the downfall of man and uplifting ; man was trying to cope his way around, either looking for a way out or trying to walk as a new creature in the Lord. We would learn for a fact that

Satan is a usurper of man's dominion and the fact he is the "Prince of Darkness" (Ephesians 2.1-3). The fallen men should be called the spiritual children of the devil (I John 3.8 10).

We were bound to sin and come to quips of our own accountability for our personal acts (I Corinthians 3.14; 2 Corinthians 5.10). We had the choice of continuing to sin, which the Lord God forbade (Romans 6.1-2), or to renounce sin and Satan the usurper and turn to the Lord Jesus Christ (Romans 6.16-23).

i

We will need to take a refresher course to renew our minds and hearts. It is very healthy to review some of the Biblical aspects for our growth and the upkeeping of the grace and knowledge of our Lord Jesus Christ (2 Peter 3.18). We need spiritual awareness or awakening to open up our realization or enlightenment within us.

We learned that in the beginning, God made man to be sinless and perfect - to be in the likeness of the Father. Man was given dominion over all creation of God's work (Genesis 1.26), but man sinned and lost his right to life and fellowship with the Heavenly Father (Genesis 3.22-24). He gave himself to sin and Satan, who took advantage of the fallen man as revenge against the Lord God, who threw Satan down from heaven for trying to usurp against the Creator (Isaiah 14.12-14).

God gave warning about the physical as well as the spiritual death prior to man's rebellious state (Romans 6.23). Thus was the punishment, and man, having no way of paying the penalty, therefore must remain dead forever. However, a promise was made after man was expelled from the perfect state (Genesis 3:15) that the salvation of man toward God would be restored. Furthermore, if man wanted to be reconciled (2 Corinthians 5.19) into the fellowship of the Father - something or someway must be done to pay the penalty.

When God gave the promise of a savior, it had to be at the right time and place, and God had chosen that right time and place. It was approximately seven to ten thousand years later! Whew! That was a long time of waiting, and God had a plan in mind for how a man could live right by giving the Mosaic Law at Mount Sinai. God knew what the law would do and would not do; however, the giving of the law was temporary until the day of Jesus Christ. The purpose of the law was to show what sin is (Romans 3.20) and how we can live right by having right judgment from right and wrong. However, through the times and trials since the giving of the law, man was not able to keep up with the law and was still under the law regardless. Man was subjected to the law even if he could not live by the law at the same time (Romans 7.7-25).

When God's time came about 400 years after Malachi, a savior was born; thus, the promise was fulfilled. God knew a substitute was necessary (Isaiah 53.4-6; I Peter 2.24). It is something that comes between the fallen man and the Lord God. This is where we meet the purpose of the brazen serpent in Numbers 21, as it is part of this book in relation to the death and atonement of Jesus Christ, which will be explained later in this book.

We will briefly go back to the historical experiences of the Hebrew nation and their involvement with Egypt at the time of Joseph before we proceed with the study of Israel's wilderness experiences. This chart will help us understand our comparison to Israel for our own enlightenment:

Pharaoh (Rameses II?) ----------------Satan (Lucifer)

The Egyptian Forces ------------------The Satanic Forces

The Hebrew Nation --------------------YOU

The Bondage --------------------------SIN

The Brazen Serpent -------------------Jesus Christ

The Promised Land -------------------Eternal Life

What and how does this chart show us in relation to Numbers 21? The experiences of Israel and ours are very much the same in comparison: "Now these things happened to them as an example, but they were written down for our instruction, on who the end of the ages has come" (I Corinthians 10.11). The wanderings of Israel are used to symbolize the defeated

Christian who fails to develop spiritual growth, strength and fruitfulness. The wilderness represents a Christian who has been able to understand what it means to die to himself and to be filled with the Spirit in Christ (Philippians 1.21; Matthew 10.38-39; Galatians 5.25; Ephesians 5.18), but later he finds that his committed life in Christ became too difficult and his spiritual growth began to level off.

We should not treat the text too lightly because all the events we see and hear that are happening today become true in every aspect of Biblical thought and in the light of the Scriptures. The most happening will occur on that certain day when and if we are ready is when the Lord Jesus Christ comes again like a thief (Revelation 3.2-3) for His church (I Thessalonians 4.16-17). This will be called "the Rapture" (a catching up, and it will happen like the twinkling of an eye - I Corinthians 15.51-53).

Before we go into the study of Numbers 21 joining the problems of Israel, let us quickly summarize ourselves as being in the same manner of behavior. Like Israel when they were under Egyptian bondage, having been slaves, we are like them the other way. We were under the bondage of Satan, bound as slaves to sin (Romans 6.14). We were children of the dark. We were

bound to the forces of evil, and there was nothing we could do to save ourselves. We had to pay the penalty for the wrong we do. Like Israel, we would cry out in despair. Oh, who would save us from going deeper and deeper (Romans 7.24)?

Let me give you an illustration: Suppose a little boy finds a lake somewhere, and no one is around. Would he, on an impulse, go in for a swim, thinking he can do it himself? He thought he could do it; however, suddenly, something happened, and he found himself in agony and despair, crying out for help. No one heard his despairing cry. No, not one! Then he goes deeper

iv

and deeper then he died. He paid the penalty because he thought he could do it, but he wasn't able to save himself. This illustration is so real and true in everyday life that this case happens all the time. The same can be applied to quicksand if you don't know where you are going through the dense part of the jungle. Here, this is the same application as any of us in the real world. Oh, who would save us? Therefore, a substitute must be met so we can become saved! That substitute is Jesus Christ. This will be explained further later in this book. So, how shall we come into Numbers 21?

Numbers 21 is a very interesting chapter. It yields some very interesting applications for our lives. As we go along in this study – each outline will deal first with the problem and then its applications at the same time – in other words, how their problems apply to us. With a special interest in Numbers 33, giving us a review of Israel's journeys from Egypt to the Promised Land. Here, especially verse 38 – it tells us that in the 21st chapter of Numbers, Israel was now in the 40th year on the first day of the fifth month (April). This was after Aaron died when Israel was nearing the promised land (Numbers 20.22-29). As we go along the wilderness journey, we will learn a type of going around in circles of doubt, perplexities, fear, and anxiety. We will summarize thus in this matter:

A. The Egyptian bondage is a type of our bondage to sin (Ephesians 2.1-2; 1.7-14; 5.1-14).

B. The Exodus from Egypt is a type of abandonment of the sinful life.

C. The Pharaoh is a type of evil force pursuing the believers.

D. The Cloud/Pillar of Fire (Numbers 14.19-20) is a type of God's divine presence protecting us.

v

A final note in this introduction is that "these things were our examples" (1 Corinthians 10.6-10).

The wilderness was part of the necessary discipline of the redeemed people. The lesson, in comparison, is to teach us the lesson of our weakness and of our dependence solely upon God (Ps.44.14).

PART ONE

Chapter 1:

The Drama of Redemption: A Brief Bird's Eye View Review Of The Egyptian Bondage Until Moses Up To The Red Sea

The call of Abraham and God's selection of Israel is revealed in the context of Genesis, Chapters 1-11. It was God's plan that certain people selected were used for a special purpose: to bring redemption to the world due to the Fall in the Garden of Eden. The selection of the Hebrews was on the basis of God's grace. God had no intention to condemn man but to redeem man from the fall of Adam.

Here in Genesis 15.13-14, the Lord God tells Abraham of the future events to take place among his descendants. It was a prophecy having been fulfilled.

A great famine arose east of Egypt, which lasted seven years, and Jacob and his family heard about Egypt's abundant food supply. At this time, Joseph was the prime minister of Egypt when Jacob and the remaining 11 sons came to Egypt seeking food aid. It was such a suitable time and moment when Joseph and his family became reunited.

It was at the Pharaoh's kindness, because of Joseph, that all his family would settle in the land of Goshen (Genesis 4.7). Genesis 46 lists the descendants of Jacob numbering 66, not counting Joseph and his two sons, making a total of 70 souls (Genesis 35.22-26). Can you imagine the tremendous growth of the Hebrews covering the land of Goshen, starting with 70 souls! It was a phenomenal growth that they multiplied, and they also became strong. Note: According to research, it was believed that the Pharaoh in Joseph's time was Amenhotep II, who was the predecessor to Thutmoses III (Exodus 2.23).

It was several years after the death of Joseph (Genesis 50.22-26) that all the 11 sons of Israel died in Egypt . There arose a king (Pharaoh) who did not know Joseph and his fame (Exodus 1.1-7). The size of the Hebrew nation scared the new Pharaoh. The population was to become a threat because of fear of invasion of Egypt due to the presence of Semitic people.

The question came to mind as to who the Pharaoh was. The Bible doesn't specifically state the names of all the Pharaohs who ruled Egypt. We had to depend on other historical and archaeological information on Egypt to determine who they were in succession. The Egyptian history is interesting, for it was part of the Cradle of Civilization. There have been some disputes that at the beginning of the Hebrew slavery, it may have been either Amenhotep I or Thutmoses I. Then, at the time of Moses, the new Pharaoh was probably Rameses II.

Nevertheless, the new Pharaoh was determined to do something about the rapid population of the Hebrew nation. He was so determined not to let that happen when and if they should invade Egypt. The Pharaoh placed them in bondage with the taskmasters over them (Exodus 1.11). Note in the same verse that two store cities, Pithom and Ramses, were built under oppression. Exodus 1.8-22 tells about the persecutions of the Hebrews. He used three methods to keep the population growth under control. Each method probably occurred several years apart.

Hard Labor (1.12) - It didn't work. The more oppressed they became, the more people began to multiply. Instructions to the midwives to kill the babies as they were born (1.17) - That didn't work because they refused to do it due to the fact that the Hebrew women were not like the Egyptian women, for they were lively.

Cast the sons of the Hebrews into the Nile River (1.22) - This method became successful.

The Hebrews sighed because of their bondage and cried for help. So we see that the Hebrews were completely innocent of their wrongs against Egypt, and they didn't seem to have any intention of Egyptian invasion . Through the years, they lost their position of honor through Joseph, whom the new Pharaoh king of Egypt didn't know and became slaves.

The prophecy given to Abraham, therefore, has become fulfilled. The Book of Exodus reveals the drama of redemption story of how the Lord

God liberated the Hebrews from their 400-year Egyptian bondage. Exodus 2.24-25 declares that God had heard their cry of affliction and became moved to meet their need.

According to the prophecy given to Abraham, the afflictions lasted 400 years, having become fulfilled. Here, we find that God's deliverance came at the most critical time when God had heard their cries.

Exodus records the birth of Moses (Chapters 1-2) and God's call to Moses (Chapters 3-4). Then, we read the confrontation between Moses as God's representative and the Pharaoh (Chapters 5-11). Chapter 12 records the Passover after the tenth and final plague against Egypt. It was such a time years later when the Pharaoh gave instructions to kill off the male babies under two years old when Moses was born. He was saved under the grace of God - for the Lord God had future plans for Moses. Moses had become a part of the royalty of Egypt when the princess pulled him out of the water and cared for him. As a result, Moses became a prince and a builder of such and such for the Pharaoh. One day, he discovered his true nationality, humbled himself, and became a slave. He later fled to Midian after killing an Egyptian and lived there for 40 years until God called him.

It was on the mountain Moses discovered God through a burning bush. He became commissioned to lead the Hebrews from the Egyptian bondage because He told Moses He heard their cries. The Lord God had prepared Moses and his brother, Aaron, for the task. We will learn that whenever God calls, He would never call anyone to do something without first preparing the task. So, it was that way with Moses. He received all the preparations necessary to meet the needs of the Hebrews.

The plagues against Egypt are listed here for information from the Book of Exodus:

1. Blood (7.14-25) - The Nile River turned to blood. Egypt worshipped the Nile, and the Nile was Egypt. The Nile supplied water, fish, and fertility. Egypt's source of life became its curse. Not only was the Nile covered with blood, but it was everywhere in Egypt.

2. Frogs (8.1-15) - The frogs were a loathsome curse, and they came out of the Nile. They multiplied very rapidly and found no way to escape from them. They invaded the land , even in all the households.

3. Lice (8.16-19) - The King James Version listed these as lice, but according to the Greek version, they are some small, harmful insects. It is said to be mosquitos or gnats (Ps.105.31). All the dust of Egypt became a massive swarm of lice or gnats. It infested Egypt.

4. Flies (8.20-32) - From now on, we see that the plagues did not harm the Hebrew slaves, only Egypt because of its scourge against the Hebrews.

5. Murrain (9.1-7) - This was a disease among the livestock on the field and everywhere, which became a major blow because the cow was considered a sacred cow. This did not affect Israel.

6. Boils (9.8-12) - The plague came without warning, and they fell upon the priesthood.

They were unable to perform their duties to the gods and found it impossible to keep themselves clean. It was a severe malady of some unknown kind of intense severity.

7. Hail (9.13-35) - This plague touched only cattle in the field and part of the crops.

8. Locusts (10.1-20) - A compromise was tried, but it was spurned, and the locusts devoured the rest of the crops.

9. Darkness (10.21-29) - Again, this plague fell upon Egypt without warning. The climax has been reached after telling the king Pharaoh of the final blow.

10. Death of the Firstborn (11.1-10) - This time, the Pharaoh did not harden is heart after the devastating death blow came upon the land of Egypt. It did not harm the Hebrews, for they were told what to do ahead of time.

The explanation of the Passover using a lamb as part of the sacrificial ceremony is very important and was one of the essential events for the Hebrews. The Passover lamb is a type of the Lord Jesus Christ who redeems with His own life-giving blood. Chapter 12 is one of the most significant chapters in the Bible, displaying the deliverance from slavery. It was a terrible judgment upon the Pharaoh and Egypt. The last plague scared Egypt, and it provided the freedom the Hebrews had long sought through the years of suffering. The plague had to do with the firstborn. We can imagine the sound of horror across the land when God sent the Angel of Death through Egypt. Wherever there was no Passover blood on the door posts and the lintel, death came.

4

The Passover lamb was to be separated from the sheep or goats and be without blemish (12.5) from the 10th to the 14th day (12.6). Then the lamb was to be killed: "And you shall take a bunch of hyssop, dip it in the blood that is in the basin, and strike the lintel (the crossbeam) and the two door posts with the blood that is in the basin (12.22). "The blood of the Passover lamb is the type of the blood of Christ who hung upon the cross and shed blood for the remission of our sins (I Peter 1.18-19); John 19.28-37). The blood on the crossbeam and the two doorposts is a picture of the bloodstained cross. Jesus is our Passover lamb who was sacrificed for us (I Corinthians 5.7).

The Lord God told Israel that his blood was a sign of salvation. Wherever the blood was applied around their doorways, wherever they were, He would pass over when He sees it (Exodus 12.13). But whenever there was no blood, death overtakes it. Hebrews 9.22 is very clear to say that without the blood of Christ, there is no forgiveness of sin. The Hebrews were instructed to partake in the Passover in remembrance of God's deliverance. Likewise, we are to do the same with the Lord's Supper in remembrance of what Jesus has done for us in His death and resurrection.

When the time came after the death of king Pharaoh's firstborn, he reluctantly released Israel from their bondage led by Moses until they had reached the Red Sea. Meanwhile, the Pharaoh began to harden his heart again and began to pursue after the Hebrews. Upon reaching the Red Sea, they had nowhere to turn to escape the Pharaoh. Once again, the Lord God had displayed his redemptive act by dividing the Red Sea so that they would cross to safety. Once they crossed with haste, the Egyptian army was behind them. The Hebrew nation crossed safely to the other side ; then, the Lord God immediately closed up the Red Sea, having destroyed the army. After crossing to the other side of Egypt for freedom as God had promised, Moses sang a song of victory to the Hebrews (Exodus 15).

Chapter 2:

The Telescopic Analytical Review of Israel's Wanderings From Egypt To The Promised Land

The Hebrews are now is a strange land, and they are about to experience their wanderings around the wilderness before finally having reached the path to the promised land after 40 years.

As we read along the books of Exodus and Numbers, we find that Israel has had quite a bit of geographical movements, as primarily described in the book of Numbers. A complete review of this is recorded in Deuteronomy 33.1-49.

The wilderness experience was nothing new to Moses, for he had had a rigor life in the wilderness for 40 years as a shepherd before the Lord God called him. The movements of Israel should be carefully scrutinized. Here is a "nation" (It was not a nation at this time until they entered the promised land.) consisting of between 2 and 3 million Hebrews. The size has increased through the years. They were compromised of an orderly arrangement spread out in accordance with divine decree around the tabernacle (Numbers 2.1-34). Each person had a proper place among the people. Everything had to be decent and in proper order.

Since the deliverance was a mighty act of the Lord God because of His love and concern and because of a promise made to Abraham, it was at Mount Sinai God made Israel His own people by entering into a covenant with them. Here, they stayed at this Mount for almost two years before they proceeded to Kadesh-Barnea. Here, we should move along with the Hebrews of all the events that took place. This is a brief outline of their wanderings during the 40-year period:

(A) From Egypt to Mount Sinai (Exodus 12.37-19.2).

(B) The Encampment at Sinai (Exodus 19.3 - Numbers 10.10).

(C) From Mount Sinai to Kadesh-Barnea (Numbers Chapters 1-12).

(D) Then, from Kadesh-Barnea, through the various wilderness wanderings and back to Kadesh-Barnea (Numbers Chapters 13-19).

(E) Finally, from Kadesh-Barnea to the River Jordan prior to entering the promised land (Numbers: Chapters 20-36).

We will now divide this up in brief of Israel in the wilderness. We will not go into details, but this outline will give you a picture of their long wanderings according to the Book of Exodus:

1. Israel was enslaved in Egypt for 400 years (1.1-12.36).

2. Israel, being freed from bondage, en route to Mount Sinai (12.37-18.27).

A. The Pursue of the Pharaoh (14.5-10)

B. At the Red Sea (14.3-15.21)

C. They arrived at Marah (15.22-26)

D. The Manna from Heaven (16.4, 14, 35)

E. The Rock (17.1-7)

F. Victory over the Amalakites (17.8-16)

3. Israel settled down at Mount Sinai (Exodus 19.1-Numbers 10.10)

A. Moses receives the Commandments (Exodus 20.3-17)

B. The Tabernacle (Exodus Chapters 26-31; 35-40)

C. The Corruption of the Golden Calf. (Exodus 32.1-35)

4. Israel en route to Kadesh-Barnea-Barnea (Numbers 10.11-12.16)

A. A Balking Bother-in-law (10.29-31)

B. A Continuing Cloud (10.34-36)

C. Murmurings Against Mixed Multitude

Fiery Plague sent as Judgment (11.1-3)

D. A Provoked Prophet (11.14-25)

E. A Deadly Diet (11.31-34)

They had a hatred against manna and turned to a diet of quail meat - the deadly plague followed.

F. A Suffering Sister (12)

Mariam was punished with leprosy for criticism against Moses and his wife.

5. Israel at Kadesh-Barnea (Numbers, Chapters 13-14)

A. A ten-man majority report about the promised land (13.31-33)

B. A two-man minority report about the Promised Land (13.30; 14.9)

C. The reaction of the people (14.2, 4)

D. The reaction of God (14.22, 29, 34, 37)

Note with interest Numbers 14.34 and Numbers 14.37 show that those who usurped the promised land would die of a plague.

6. Israel now going from Kadesh-Barnea to the Eastern Bank (Numbers, Chapters15-36).

7. Israel is now at the Eastern Bank just prior to the Promised Land

It is worth noting that when they first arrived at Kadesh-Barnea after spending several months at Mount Sinai , they began to dispute about the Promised Land. Thus - from there, they began their 40 years of circling the wilderness. Numbers 21 records their 40th year prior to entering the Promised Land.

So, we see that as we join the Hebrews, we are like them as we try to grow in the grace and knowledge of our Lord Jesus Christ (2 Peter 3.18). They had the weakness and sin of man while the Lord God had the strength and grace upon them. They were filled with disbelief and discontentment, and the Lord God had shown His faithfulness and patience.

While we go along with them, we find that the Hebrews had murmured from time to time. Each time they murmured, the Lord God had to deal with them. Now the question is: What does it mean when you murmur like the Hebrew people did to deserve judgment from the Lord God? It expresses a low , distinct feeling with a low whisper of criticism; however, this type of murmuring would lead you into trouble with others who may lose respect for you.

The Lord God's anger became provoked, that He became tired of their disbelief (Numbers 14.11). Numbers 14.31 is worthy to note. Of all the murmurings, the complaint about the promised land was the most serious situation when they showed fear and doubts, which eventually led them to their 40-year wilderness wanderings. The murmurings and the reasons for each are listed here for information. They complained 12 times during their journeys, which was the chief problem and had become their favorite pastime.

1. At the Red Sea (Exodus 14.11-12)

    The complaint: The Pursue of the Egyptians.

2. At Mariah (Exodus 15.23-24)

    The complaint: The water was very bitter.

3. In the Wilderness of Sin (Exodus 16.1-5)

    The complaint: Against Moses and Aaron for hunger (2 reasons listed in 4 and 5)

4. In connection with manna (Exodus 16.20 and 16.27)

5. They didn't listen to Moses's instructions.

6. At Rephidim (Exodus 17.1-3)

    The complaint: Lack of water

7. At Mount Horeb (Exodus 32)

The complaint: Not seen Moses for a period of time; corrupt themselves

8. At Taberah (Numbers 12.1)

The complaint: Mariam and Aaron against Moses's marriage

9. The complaint against mixed marriages (Numbers 11.4)

10. At Kadesh-Barnea (Numbers 14)

11. In Kadesh-Barnea (Numbers 20.2-11)

12. Having to encompass the land of Edom (Numbers 21.4)

Notes: #1. The Red Sea is a picture of death and resurrection

(Death to sin and the old life into newness and victory)

#4. The Manna typifies Christ as the bread from heaven (John 6.48-51).

There are ten plagues in the Book of Numbers:

1. Fire - 11.1-3

2. Sickness - 11.4-35

3. Leprosy - 12.1-16

4. Death - 14.28-35

5. Sickness - 13.31-33; 14.37

6. Earthquake - 16.1-3, 29-35

7. Fire - 16.1-3, 34-35

8. Sickness - 16.41-50

9. Serpents - 21.5-9

10. Sickness - 25.1-9

There are ten murmurings against Moses:

1. Water – Exodus 15.24-26

2. Food – Exodus 16.2-3

3. Water – Exodus 17.3-7

4. Jealousy – Numbers 12.1-16

5. Fear/Cowardice – Numbers 14.2-38

6. Jealousy – Numbers 16.1-35

7. Bitterness – Numbers 16.41-50

8. Jealousy – Numbers 17.1-13

9. Water – Numbers 17.1-13

10. Food – Numbers 21.4-9

Notes:

Why 40 years? God gave them one year of wandering in the wilderness for each day the spies spent checking out the land of Canaan (Numbers 14.32-35).

The numbering of Hebrews since their time in Egypt was approximately 2 million, according to Exodus 12.37 and Numbers 1.46. Note the phrase "besides women and children" would suggest a total company of about 2 million.

The first census of the Hebrews is recorded in Numbers 1.1-40, and the second census of the new generation is recorded in Numbers 26.1-51. The position of the tribes of the Hebrews is

recorded in Numbers 2.1-34 as shown here:

NORTH

Naphtali Dan Asher Manasseh The Tabernacle Zebulon

WEST

Ephraim (The Levites) Judah

EAST

Benjamin Issachar Simeon Reuben Gad

SOUTH

The journeys of Israel are recorded in Numbers 33.1-49 through chapter 42, and the names of the camping places of the Hebrews are recorded in Numbers 33.19-26.

On the bank of the Jordan River Moses delivers three sermons (1st Sermon – Deuteronomy 1-4; 2nd Sermon – Deuteronomy 5-26; 3rd Sermon – Deuteronomy 27-30), issues a challenge to Joshua (Deuteronomy 31.14-29), composes a song (Deuteronomy 32), pronounces a blessing upon the individual tribes (Deuteronomy 33), and departs for heaven (Deuteronomy 34). The sermons were related to sin, judgment, intercession and renewal.

PART TWO:
THE EXPOSITORY PERSPECTIVE OF NUMBERS 21.4-35 IN RELATION TO THE SPIRITUAL JOURNEY OF THE LIFE AND TIMES OF THE CHRISTIAN IN COMPARISON

Chapter 1:

Doubts and Disobedience: Failing Faith (Numbers 21.4-5)

"From Mount Hor, they set out by the way to the Red Sea, to go around the land of Edom. And the people became impatient on the way. And the people spoke against God and against Moses, "Why have you brought us up out of Egypt to die in the wilderness? For there is no food and no water, and we loathe this worthless food."

Here, from these verses, we are dealing with failing faith. They have been through this on a number of occasions, and each time, judgment befalls them from the Lord God is dealt with. This chapter study fits well in a divine way in which we will go as we go along with the Israelites in their doubts and disobedience.

If we look carefully at these verses, we will see why they spoke against God and Moses and the later effect that came to them in the next chapter of this book. We can rewrite this in a much longer narrative and interpret it to make the story more interesting. It is obvious that it is a short review of the previous experience they had encountered before they started to murmur again about the food and water. To get the full story, we will have to go back to Numbers 20.

It was well into the 40th year, around April (Jewish calendar of the first month of the year), when the Israelites returned to Kadesh-Barnea and camped there awhile. They were getting close to the Promised Land. They were situated in the Wilderness of Sin on the edge of the Moabite Territory. We see there a glimpse of the death and burial of Moses's sister, Miriam.

Then, we find that Israel started to complain again upon their arrival. This will be their 11th complaint. This not only provoked God to anger (Numbers 14.11) but angered Moses. They have said it before, and it was always the same problem. They complained about the lack of water.

We see here that Moses disobeyed God again when instructed to strike the rock only once to produce water. Moses lost his temper and stuck it twice. He has done that once years before (Ex.17.5-7), and once again, this did not please the Lord God. Moses became very weary of Israel's failure to trust in the Lord God and asked about the miracles He had performed since leaving Egypt. This place was called Meribah, and God called it the Water of Quarreling (Numbers 20.13) because of the contention and fault-finding of the Hebrews. Not only these reasons, but they also tempted and tried the patience of the Lord. Nevertheless, Moses's behavior failed to honor or display trust toward the Lord God. The rock mitten typifies the Lord Jesus Christ to indicate that He was once smitten, not having to be smitten (crucified) again (I Corinthians 10.4). Moses is told he will not enter the promised land. We can imagine how Moses felt, but he had to accept God's chastisement. Furthermore, here is and old generation that has nearly passed away, and they still have the tendency to rebel. There is that stiff discipline to face - but the new generation has yet to learn when to obey the one true God, and these are the ones who will enter the promised land.

As the story goes, according to Numbers 21.1-3 - Canaan, that land of milk and honey, was not too afar off. The most probable way to get there was to go through the land of Edom. Moses sends his messengers to the king of Edom to request permission to go through the land with a promise not to go astray on their territory or else pay for whatever has been taken or damaged.

The Edomite king refused the request, and the Edomites were armed and ready for attack and stood across the only way to Canaan. So, Israel avoided it and turned south again and then went east.

There was an obvious reason for the futile negotiations with Edom. We find from earlier history that Edom was Israel's brother (Genesis 35.1-15; 36.1). The Edomites are descended from Esau (Genesis 36.1), and the Israelites descended from Jacob. According to the Genesis story, it had to do with the birthright Jacob took from Esau, and Esau became very bitter and was filled with hatred against Jacob. However, they had later come to terms with reconciliation years before, but obviously, they had not been accepted by the descendants. Nevertheless, the Edomites refused to allow Israel to go through the land regardless of the reasonable request of Moses to go through the land of Edom. What transformed Edom to become enemies of Israel regardless of the terms of reconciliation years before between Esau and Jacob is not known.

Then they went on to Kadesh-Barnea and came to Mount Hormah, having not been too far from Edom. They camped there, and the Lord told Moses it was time to take the life of his brother Aaron. He was also told that Aaron would not be able to enter the promised land because they both rebelled at Meribah. He was instructed to bring along Eleazar, Aaron's son so that the priesthood would be turned over to him. When all that was done, Israel mourned for thirty days.

We will now proceed to Numbers 21.1-3. Here, we find that the children of Israel were about to break camp at Mount Hormah in Kadesh-Barnea when they became involved in warfare against the Canaanites. What we are looking at is their first recorded victory. These verses give us a brief account of their victory over King Arad the Canaanite (Numbers 21.1--3). Israel was beginning to taste the experience of warfare for the first time to come to quip for protection and began to fight back and utterly destroyed all the cities.

The Canaanite king who lived in the Negev had heard that Israel came by the way of the spies. Here, this means that they were going the same way the spies went in to spy out the land 40 years before after having crossed the Red Sea from Egypt. However, they were coming along the road to Atharim, and the king attacked Israel and took some prisoners. Israel prayed to the Lord for deliverance. The result was a victory for Israel because they were defeated by the Amalekites and Canaanites a generation before (Numbers 14.41-45).

We are now entering the study of our spiritual journey, starting with Numbers 21.4-5. We find that Israel had to travel from Mount Hormah along the route to the Red Sea to go around Edom after the king of Edom refused to give them permission to go through their land, which was the easiest way to enter the promised land (Numbers 20.14-21). According to verse 4, they were compassing the land of Edom. From Kadesh, Israel had intended to march through the country of the Edomites and go northward to the River Jordan, which they would then cross to enter the promised land. But the Edomite King and the Edomites held the old hatred against Israel would not permit them to pass through.

Verse 5 - Somewhere along the way, they started to become "discouraged because of the way" (King James Version). To become discouraged, in this case, does not mean to become depressed - letting yourself down , but to become impatient. They became very frustrated and ran out of patience.

Verse 6 - They started to question Moses, wondering why they were still going in the same direction again. They were wondering why they were still going in circles. They were wondering when they were going to settle down. They started to complain again about the manna and the lack of water. We will learn that this is their 12th complaint and probably be the last prior to reaching the Promised Land. They showed their outbreak of anger and disgust and being impudent and blasphemous were something "more substantial" of their behavior toward Moses. We will remember that the manna was given from the day they crossed over the Red Sea, and it is no wonder they hated the heavenly bread and thought that it was contemptible (Exodus 16.14-22). This is the same complaint they have made throughout their wilderness journeys. Later in the next round of the chapter, we will find out how the Lord God judged their behavior.

Here, we see that Israel had lost their faith in trusting in the Lord God and Moses in a moment's seconds. It was a loss of self-confidence , their failure to keep up with faith before we move on. The question here: What is faith? It is showing complete trust or confidence in someone or something. It is a strong belief in God or in the doctrines of religion based on spiritual apprehension rather than proof. From the scriptures of Hebrews 11.1: "Now faith is the assurance of things hoped for, the conviction of things not seen." This is belief, trust and loyalty to a person or thing. It deals with security and hope in God as revealed in Jesus Christ. As the Israelites displayed their behavior, they showed a burst of anger without thinking about what the Lord God had to go through. Moses had to bear it all, and we can imagine the weary look on his face when he had to bear their angry behavior. They had shown their distrust in the leadership of Moses no matter how hard he tried to serve to the best of his ability.

We are like that of the Israelites. Satan was at work, causing their failures and ours. The Bible tells us that Satan began his evil ways, starting with Adam and Eve in the Garden of Eden . We have heard and seen how some church members would show distrust in their own spiritual leaders, but this also affects the Lord God because they were chosen by God to serve His kingdom. We leaders have faults, and we all are human beings like those accusers. I have experienced such against me through my ministerial years.

One day, somewhere in South Carolina, a woman was hurrying home from work because she was expecting some guests for the evening. As she drove along her familiar route, she came upon a train crossing, and a long line of cars were bumper to bumper ahead of her. She knew she would not make it if she had to wait. She knew a shortcut, being unaware of the construction ahead.

She came upon construction at work, and she proceeded slowly. At about the same time, a huge construction tractor fell sideways from a sloping hillside, having lost its balance. It fell right on top of her car with the woman in it, crushing her to death instantly.

It is a sad story, isn't it? We like to make short cuts of all sorts, but we don't know what lies ahead of us. We don't know how the shortcuts would affect us or the danger of it. There is not even a shortcut to heaven either, for the Bible tells us that there are two roads to take: one is narrow, but few make it, while the other road is wide, only to meet destruction

(Matthew 7.13-14). When we take a certain test, there are no possible shortcuts like Algebra, for example. We may learn some shortcuts to solving an algebraic problem, but when we take a test, we are expected to know how to solve a problem without any shortcuts. But if we use a shortcut, we will be marked wrong.

In John 14.6 Jesus said no one comes to the Father except by Him. What He is saying is that is that there is no short cut to the Father except through Him. This is the reason why Jesus went to the cross for our sins.

It is the same way with us. We may go on the wrong track if we take a shortcut whenever we try to find a solution. Remember to take one step at a time, and everything will work out. On the other hand, if we decide to take the shortcut, we are likely to have problems and may come up with some failures. We don't and cannot expect miracles overnight. If you will recall that the Israelites wanted to go through Edom, but instead, they had to go the long way around. To go through Edom was like a shortcut. I believe the Lord God planned this to test the Israelites. Even if we are trying to grow in our daily Christian lives by absorbing the grace and knowledge of our Lord Jesus Christ (2 Peter 3.18). It is impossible to take shortcuts in our growth because we are like babes, and we have to go one step at a time to do things right. We have to be patience and have courage no matter how long it takes (Psalm 27.14; Philippians 4.13; Psalm 40.1).

The Israelites displayed an outbreak of anger and disgust despite not only the fact of going out of the way but they also complained of the lack of food and water. They were becoming tired of the "games they were playing." They felt like pawns. What? They didn't understand, or we didn't, that the Lord God is the only source of life to many, but we would blame God or our leaders for not only theirs but our remorse feelings for trying to bring "death to the nation" going around in circles without hardly any food and water.

In the Gospel of Luke, 12.29-31 says that we should not seek what we shall eat or drink, nor be doubtful of mind. For all these things do the nations of the world seek after. It also says that the Father knows our needs ahead of time but rather seeks first the kingdom of God, and He will provide (Matthew 6.33). Do you believe this? If you do - then start trusting in Him daily, and do not be confused with yourself.

Like the Israelites, we have failed to absorb in our hearts and minds the saving power of God since our bondage with Egypt (Satan). We were experiencing spiritual blindness toward understanding the will of God in our lives. We have failed what God had required of us - that is obedience. God knew what was in the heart of man, and He was well prepared to deal with the problems of man, and they were well justified.

If we have failed God, then we have failed the test of endurance (James 1.12a). We have become weakened in that Satan took advantage of using our failures against God. Satan would find out our weaknesses and begin to make our weaknesses a target of neglecting salvation so great (Hebrews 2.3a). Therefore, we are still going in circles. Like Israel, they moved in circles only to come back to the same place - Kadesh to Kadesh.

Is this the picture of your life? How much progress have you made in your spiritual things of life? The wilderness was part of the necessary discipline of the redeemed people. The psalmist in Chapter 44.1-4 says to teach them (or us) the lesson of their weakness and of dependence solely upon God. The Apostle Paul stresses the fact they have become examples of the Israelites' experience for us in 1 Corinthians 10.6-13).

I don't believe in Mythology. I enjoy watching movies or reading books involving mythology; however, there are lessons to be taught. There are some applications we can use to apply to our lives. There is one I would like to share - the story of Achilles' Heel. There is an application of this story that can apply to ourselves.

As the story goes , When he was a baby, his mother took him to the River Styx and dipped him in the river in order that he receive immortality. However, his mother didn't dip him all the way, leaving only the spot where she held - at the heel. As time went by, he became a hero in many of the wars of Greece because he was immortal.

One day, he was at war against Troy, where the beautiful princess Helen was. Paris, her lover, was there to fight against Achilles from the fortress. They didn't know what they were up against, even though they knew about Achilles' immortality. Somehow or the other, Paris knew something about his immortality. He had an idea about his weak spot. Paris aimed his crossbow at the ready at the right time and shot the arrow at Achilles' heel. When it hit home - at the right spot of his weakness – Achilles fell to his death. Thus, Troy won the battle.

Sound familiar? I Peter 5.8-9 says: "Humble yourselves, therefore, under the mighty hand of God so at the proper time he may exalt you, casting all your anxieties on him, because he cares for you. Be sober-minded, be watchful. Your adversary, the devil, prowls around like a roaring lion, seeking someone to devour. Resist him, firm in your faith, knowing that the same kinds of suffering are being experienced by your brotherhood throughout the world."

Here, Satan is like that - seeking out our weakness or our weak spot. Once he finds it, we will then fall away from the fellowship of the Father. What sort of weak spots would Satan be looking for in our lives? They could be anything. Satan doesn't care what it is, so as long as he can try to tempt us to go astray , we will have to be aware and be ready to stand against him, as Peter pointed out in these verses. The most dangerous part of our Christian living is the Apostasy. It is happening all the time. I would encourage you to eat all of the Book of Jude relating to this problem.

Another example is from 1 Peter 5.7. It says to cast all your anxiety on God because God the Father cares about you (New International Version). When we have found Christ in our lives, we become free of sin (Ephesians 1.7; 1 John 1.7-9). Then, while we try to show up, we would find some difficulties in adjusting to our new Christian life. We have allowed Satan to take small control of our lives after he discovered our weaknesses. We would then make our weaknesses to go completely out of control.

Do not confuse yourself, but be very diligent in trusting Christ Jesus. Satan is truly hard at work trying to usurp our Christian living. This is exactly what happened in the Garden of Eden when he discovered the weakness of Adam and Eve (Genesis 3). We must not get out of the law of gravity of God's truth when Satan tries to confuse us with some principle values not contrary to Biblical concepts.

I would like to cite one example shared with me as it is based on fact. A Baptist church had a revival planned, and a guest evangelist was invited to preach for that week. The first night of the revival, the evangelist, as usual, like most preachers would do, is to pray first before the beginning of the sermon. As he prayed - all of a sudden, he began to speak in tongues, thus startling the congregation. They became confused. The Bible states that there be an interpreter among us to be able to interpret what he said, and if there be none, we should let him be silent (2 Corinthians 14.1-25). Fortunately, there was an interpreter in the congregation who understood the language because he was a missionary. The interpreter went up to the pulpit and shook him up, causing him to be silent. He announced that the evangelist was speaking in an African language he understood in the name of Satan! Thereby, the church canceled the revival. Speaking in tongues was a dramatic miracle that helped with the beginning of the Jerusalem church and thus began the ministry of the church in spreading the power of the gospel (Acts 2.1-4). This is different compared to one who speaks in tongues. There were two other instances relating to speaking in tongues, but they were also different for good reasons (Acts 10.44-46; 19.1-6).

This is one of those situations in which we do not need to be involved such as this because we have Christ in us. We do not need to experience speaking in tongues as some churches are practicing it, nor do we need to experience the baptism of the Holy Spirit (the second blessing, as some charismatic churches describe). When we are saved, the Holy Spirit is immediately in us. If Jesus said he would be with us always (Matthew 28.19), then the Spirit is with us for Christ , and the Spirit is one and the same as God and Christ. All three are one!! If we want the Holy Spirit - all we have to do is pray for the infilling of His power (Ephesians 1.17). He already indwells in us (Romans 8.9-10).

I will not venture any further to explain the touchy charismatic subjects as they will require exhaustive material to cover. I would suggest you buy a book on these things to be able to understand these concepts so as not to confuse yourself. This is what the Apostle Paul was trying to straighten out the serious contentions and strides among the Corinthian Christians when he received word of their problems of confusion from Chloe (1 Corinthians 1.11). He became disappointed and sad-hearted about their failures and immaturity in their unity. Then he went on to give them advices, treating them in a way a father would treat his son for misbehaviour (1 Corinthians 7.1a). The Corinthians were like the Israelites in the wilderness. We, in modern times, are like that.

One day, I witnessed someone about Jesus and learned that the person experienced speaking in tongues and was baptized in the Holy Spirit. I was told that if I had not experienced both, I would not go to heaven. My friend - do not be deceived!! No where in the Bible tells me otherwise. The only way to heaven is through Jesus, for He says: "I am the way, the truth, and the life. No man comes to the Father but by me (John 14.6).

An old house painted black stood on a street in San Francisco called "the Church of Satan" was formed by its "high priest," Anton Szandor LaVey, in 1966 when he shook the world of Christianity with a new doctrine: "God Is Dead!" It caused a great deal of calamity and confusion, leading to apostasy among the churches. Many have left their church as a result, with a deep shadow over their minds. It was a triumph for those who didn't believe in God. Another "church" dedicated to Satanic worship was headed by Arthur J. Slavin in Toledo, Ohio. He was formerly and essential fixture for the Temple Bat Yam community.

Since the establishment of Devil worship, it has long expanded its activities to major cities in America. I came across one in St. Augustine, Florida, during the latter part of the 1970s. Through the power of the Holy Spirit, I was able to convert a few to the saving grace of our Lord Jesus Christ.

What about witchcraft? Astrology? Other occults? The Bible speaks against such not contrary to the scriptures (Deuteronomy 18.9-22, 13.1-5; Isaiah 8.19-29; Ephesians 6.12; Colossians 2.16-19). Witchcraft has long been practiced; however, the practice of witchcraft during Biblical times differs from the Medieval times, and today's self-styled witches usually resemble the ancient concept more than that of the Medieval Ages.

In the Biblical narrative, King Saul of Israel killed himself after failing to depend on God for help when he went to visit the witch of Endor (1 Samuel 28.3-25). God was very angry for such behavior and permitted judgment against Saul. We find in Isaiah 28.15 that a person can be considered to be a person who had sold his/her soul to Satan in exchange for magical powers. They would be considered dangerous.

Witchcraft is all over the world, having as many as at least 5 to 10 million believing witches practicing today. This may sound unbelievable and as astounding, but it is true. There are about 8,000 or more witches meeting regularly in small groups throughout England. In Manhattan, New York, there are over 1,500 believing witches, most notably in Salem,

Massachusetts, famous for witchcraft. They would meet monthly, at the time of the full moon, and at eight or more other festivals called Sabbats throughout the year. Witchcraft to them. It is a "religion" – Satan's religion that denies or distorts the Bible, ignores or perverts the doctrine of Christ and offers no deliverance from the guilt and power of sin.

Satan is an angel of light (2 Corinthians 11.14-15). You can be deceived by his followers who can transform themselves to bring you into very deceptive ways before you know what's happening, especially the cults. Satan is very clever and has many deceptive tactics and uses his followers within the church to bring about some controversial issues that will cause divisions and split-ups within the church. This is what happened with the Corinthian church during Paul's time. He is capable of stirring up strifes and enmities among God's people. Is God to be divided? The Bible says God is not the God of confusion. We are familiar with this motto: "United We Stand; Divided We Fall." Are we this? There are times when we are in that situation. No, we should never be in this situation. Whoever thought up this motto – we are surely misled in using this motto. If we are to stand united if we are to be one in Christ (Galatians 3.28); Philippians 2.2). So, who has the mind of Christ (Romans 2.16)?

"O foolish Galatians! Who has bewitched you? It was before your eyes that Jesus Christ was publicly portrayed as crucified?" (Galatians 3.1). Does the Bible say not to have no fellowship with the unfruitful works of darkness, but, rather, reprove them (Ephesians 5.11 King James Version).

So, you see, my friend, we are still going in circles, hopping around from one place to another. Would you dare to start doubting about God? Romans 14.23 says, "But whoever has doubts is condemned if he eats, because the eating is not from faith. For whatever does not proceed from faith is a sin. James 1.6 says, "But let him ask in faith, with no doubting, for the one who doubts is like a wave of the sea that is driven and tossed by the wind." Do not be deceived! Do not believe in a lie! The Bible says if Christ arose from the dead having victory over death, then it would be logical to believe that He, the living God, is alive again so that we can live eternally. Even the devils believed also (James 2.19).

Therefore, if your God is dead, try mine! Therefore, he who pleases God best and trusts Him the most.

In summarization:

1. Failing faith
2. No shortcuts
3. Achilles' heel
4. Devil worship and witchcraft
5. Casting all your cares

Chapter 2:

The Fiery Serpents: God Judges Broken Law (Numbers 21.6)

"Then the Lord sent fiery serpents among the people, and they bit the people so that many people of Israel died."

Romans 8.13 says: "For if you live according to the flesh, you will die, but if through the Spirit you put to death the deeds of the body, you will live (Modern English Version)." Here, we find that God judges broken law. He was watching and hearing everything that was going on. We cannot run and hide like Adam and Eve in the Genesis story of the fall of sin (Genesis 3.1-24). God the Father knows what is going on with your life and what is in the heart of man. Like Adam and Eve, we cannot escape from the supernatural God by His attributes. Let us look at His attributes for a minute. He is everywhere present (omnipresent); He is all-knowing(omniscient); and He is all-powerful (omnipotent).

Being omnipresent, there is no pace where God the Father is not present. The presence of God permeates all space, time, and matter. David, the psalmist, expresses that the presence of God is almighty to the extent that He extends to all space at all times (Psalm 139.1-12). David emphasizes by a question that God is everywhere that he may go. Verse 8 begins a list of theses spaces. The first is heaven – God is there. The second is hell – God is also there.

Being omniscient, David describes God's infinite knowledge of Him. David says God has searched him and had known him (Psalm 139.1-4). He emphasizes that God knows him completely. Does God know everything about us? Does God know things about us that we may not be aware of? Does God use His all-knowing power to minister to us? In Psalm 139.5-6, David becomes aware of God's infinite knowing and declares that God is in absolute control of all that affects his life and ours as well.

Being omnipotent by that it means the power of God to execute His will. This does not mean that God does everything. The Bible teaches that God does not lie, change, or die. The omnipotence of God is expressed in Jeremiah 32.17-19. God is mighty and able to execute His divine will. Chapter 32 is the testimony and witness of Jeremiah while he was in prayer regarding his investment. Nothing is too wonderful or impossible for God when Jeremiah declares, "Nothing is too hard for you."

Verses 18-19 show the kind of power God has. Jeremiah had the knowledge of the ways of God's power. Is God able to maintain His justice in the lives of the people? His justice throughout the world? Do we have any reason to fear justice when we serve an all-powerful God, even when His power is used to display His love and care for His people? Verse 19 is a summary of verses 17-18, declaring both the power and care of God, reflecting His ability to accomplish what He wills. What God has done and what He will do is displayed in His ever-omnipotence.

We will learn from the attributes of God that God executes judgment. What do we mean when we say that God judges the broken law? In reality, it means not being able to put complete trust in Him and broken fellowship (1 John 1.3, 6). During these times and trials since leaving Egypt and throughout history, God has judged Israel's behavior with severity and death.

God can be patient, but at the same time, His patience can try us when we arouse His anger and wrath (Isaiah 13.13; Ezekiel 5.13; Ezekiel 20.8-20; Psalm 2.5a; Romans 9.22). The anger of the Lord was felt, and He was not pleased with Israel's murmurings that the Lord would unexpectedly send fiery serpents among the people. Here, this was divine judgment for a reason for the sake of prophecy to be fulfilled. We are to expect the unexpected. We are to be prepared

ahead of time when we face trials and tribulations or else feel the wrath of God. Oh, who would deliver us from the wrath of God (1 Thessalonians 1.10). We find that God deals with us in a very mysterious way and can be unexpected , whether it be a tragedy or not or whatever it may befall us.

The Book of Numbers narrative does not specifically describe the type of snakes, but they were described as fiery. They were for real – just as God had created the heavens and the earth. However, they were also very venomous, and many people of Israel died. The death was not slow. It was not known how long the judgment of the fiery serpents lasted. It is also not known how many died in one day, two days, or one week. We will also note that the number of people is not mentioned. We find that the Apostle Paul makes mention of the number of people who died from the terrible plague. We read from his writings in 1 Corinthians 10.6-12 in relation to Israel's experience of the fiery serpents. He says these things took place as examples for us in comparison. He says in verse 8 that 23,000 persons fell to the plague in a single day. Now we know how long it took according to his writings. We also find another instance of this number from Numbers 25.9. Here, it says 24,000. The Apostle Paul must have figured this number as 23,000, leaving 1,000 from another incident. However, the case may be – we know is that they were numbered in the thousands.

There has been some discernment in our minds, wondering why God does these things not only to Israel but to everyone. We say that He is a loving God, for He is love (1 John 4.7-12) yet brings death. Yes, it is hard to comprehend, but for good reasons. Not only is God the God of love but of judgment also. We have to remember the holiness of the Lord God as His holiness is displayed in Genesis, Chapters 1-5. Not only is His holiness displayed from the beginning of

Genesis, but throughout history. He is without any form of sin or defilement. It goes back to the time in the Garden of Eden when sin entered the Garden of Eden when sin entered that perfect place. The Lord God declared that physical and spiritual death is involved when we have broken the divine law – to trust and obey His Will! Later in the life of Abraham, a promise was made in the Abrahamic Covenant that God the Father would bless those who blessed Abraham and cursed those who cursed him – and they were carried out! (Genesis 11).

Let's take a look at Psalm 2.1. The Psalmist says: "Why do the nations rage and the peoples plot in vain?" And also, in verse 5: "Then He will speak to them in His wrath, and terrify them in His fury…" We can rage all we want, all in vain, blaming God for all the things happening around us. We would also often wonder why God permitted this. When we do, we will have the taste of His chastisement. We read from Hebrews 12.5-11 that the Lord God does chastise us for our failures, and it is for our own good. To become chastised means we can become better and well-disciplined.

It shows proof of God's genuine love (agape) and care relationship for us (Hebrews 12.6-8). It helps us to become more obedient and to trust Him more (v.9). We also learn from it not to make the same mistakes again (v.10) so that we can be a part of God's holiness (v.14; 1 Pet.1.16). By that, we become more consecrated and sanctified. We become pure and perfect in Christ, having that divine enlightenment. Then , verse 11 of Hebrews says that after having been chastised, we will produce the peaceable fruit of righteousness in our lives. What did the Hebrew writer mean by that? Was he referring to the fruit of the Spirit, from which comes the spiritual place in all aspects of being a well-rounded Christian that the Lord God expects us to be? If so, we may find them from Galatians 5.22-23. Here, under this circumstance, we have the renewing of the mind in the Spirit by putting on the new man (Ephesians 4.22-24).

The author has shared some testimonies of those he had tried to share Jesus Christ. They had come to know the Lord through the conviction of the Holy Spirit a few years later. One came through a near tragedy. So, we can see that God does throngs His way in mysterious ways.

God is a God of judgment. His ways are established, and if we violate His ways, we will require His judgment. In Egypt, the Lord God had seen His people treated unjustly. The Pharaoh dealt with the Hebrews very cruelly. He was in violation of human rights, which wasn't thought of in those days like now in our modern times. The agreements with Joseph when his family was reunited were violated by the Pharaoh, who did not know Joseph. God had to deal with Egypt with His divine judgment. It also meant the redemption of Israel and for the faithful. We should not fear His judgments only if we remain faithful to Him by trusting in Him through obedience.

The Lord God brought judgment against the whole world at the time of Noah by sending the flood (Gen.6). Chapters 6-11 show His judgment beginning with Noah to the time of Abraham. There is no vindictiveness in

God's judgment. He is just deeply grieved about the rebellion of mankind (6.6). He also brought judgment against Sodom and Gomorrah when He first got Lot and several others out (Genesis 19.1-29). He destroyed the cities that were filled with evil and sin to the core by fire. We are slow to learn about God's righteous judgment. Another example is God's judgment against Ananias and Sapphira for lying and cheating against the Holy Spirit (Acts 5.1-10). The sin displayed was in misrepresentation against the Lord God. The case of Ananias and Sapphira was first against God and the church; secondly, because it was through the body of believers, they became hurt by the misrepresentation toward the Lord. The reason for

God's judgment is to purify the believers from that sin which had jeopardized their Christian living. In reality, God's purpose is to judge the sin of mankind and to restrain its serious effects on the world. At this time of my writing this book, everything in this world up to this point is in shambles and in turmoil. We can see God through the power of the Holy Spirit. He is continuing to judge us. Like Adam in the Garden of Eden, he runs to hide (Genesis 3.8-10), and Cain makes excuses about what happened to his brother Abel (Genesis 4.9-12). Are we like Adam and Cain?

The Bible reveals that there are about seven separate judgments, and they are different in time, place and purpose. Everyone, from Adam to the last man on Earth, will stand before the Lord Jesus Christ to be judged. They all have one thing in common: The Lord Jesus Christ is the Judge. One of these refers to the judgment of the true believer's self. The believer is to judge self or be judged and disciplined by the Lord Jesus Christ (1 Corinthians 11.31; Hebrews 12.5-7). From the viewpoint of 1 Corinthians 11:31, the idea here is not to the point of judging others lest you be judged (Matthew 7.1-5; Luke 6.37). It has to do with personal self of the believer. It has to do with his daily living and influence. It is self-examination by searching yourself out by means of going to the Lord God in prayer for the purging of your self sin in your life. This involves self-sacrifice , which is "holy, acceptable to God, which is your reasonable service" (Romans 12.1 King James Version). Not only that, it also means not to be conformed to this world but to be transformed with a renewed mind (Romans 12.2). However, in that same verse, it states that we have to prove what is good and acceptable and perfect will of God. This means to deny yourself (Mark 8.34-38). In other words – renounce yourself; it is replacing self with Christ-life (Colossians 3.4). It is losing your own life in Christ (Galatians 2.20; Matthew 16.25-26).

The seven judgments of scripture are shared here for your information. Among the many scriptural judgments mentioned, these are especially noted with specific significance. These are:

1. The Judgment of the Believer's Sins (John 5.25;12.31)

    (The sins of the believer have already been judged in Christ on the cross.)

2. The Judgment of the Believer's Self (1 Corinthians 11.27-32)

(The believer is to judge self or be judged and disciplined by the Lord Jesus Christ.)

3. The Judgment of the Believer's Works (2 Corinthians 5.10)

    (All believers must appear at the judgment seat of Chris where their works are to be judged.)

4. The Judgment of Nations at the return of Christ (Matthew 25.31-46)

    (All nations are to be judged at the Second Coming of Christ.)

5. The Judgment of Israel at the Return of Christ (Ezekiel 20.37)

    (Israel has come under many cycles of discipline.)

6. The Judgment of Angels after the 100 years (Jude 6)

    (Those angels are already in prison awaiting Judgment Day.)

7. The Judgment of the Wicked Dead and Alive (Revelation 21)

    (The wicked, dead and alive, will be judged at he Great White Throne.)

Of all these seven judgments, we would be concerned with connection to this book would be the judgment of the believer's self-judgment based on 1 Corinthians 11.31-32.

8. It involves the believer's walking in the light (I John 1.7).
9. It will occur during this life (Ephesians 4.22-32; Colossians 3.5-17).
10. It will occur in the believer's own life (Romans 8.1-16; Hebrews 12.5-11).
11. Obedience is the basis of God and His Word (James 1.22-25).
12. The chastisement would be the result from the Lord (Hebrews 12.5-11).

(The Book of Hebrews reveals that the judgment deals with the believer as a son during his spiritual journey.)

Therefore, we can see what we are up against. We have abused our Christian living for not being the body of Christ. Which temple are we? So says the Apostle Paul (1 Corinthians 3.16-17). Furthermore, he says that we should not defile our own bodies. Not only that, but in the same chapter, he says we are as carnally-minded having been fed with milk. In other words – he is saying that we have become immature in our growth, walking after the things of the flesh (Rom.8.5). Paul emphasized from Romans 8 that to be carnally-minded is enmity against God because we are not being subject to the law of God. We are not to live in the flesh but to be in the Spirit. The Spirit is life because of the righteousness of God (Romans 8.10).

In summarization, we have the following:

1. The fiery serpents
2. God's judgment
3. The seven judgments

Chapter 3:

You Must Confess Your Sins!! (Numbers 21.7)

And the people came to Moses and said, "We have sinned, for we have spoken against the Lord and against you. Pray to the Lord that he take away the serpents from us." So Moses prayed for the people.

When Israel began to realize what was happening when God sent the fiery serpents , fear came upon them, and they went to Moses for forgiveness. Fear took a good grip on the children of Israel. When it did, they were sore and afraid – took a dire toll on them – for the worse. They thought that they could get away with it. It is easy to admit your guilt when fears strike at you when you become chastised. The Bible says we must fear the Lord God (Deuteronomy 6.13; 10.12; 32.12; Joshua 4.24; 24.14; 1 Samuel 12.14, 24; Psalm 2.11; 19.9; 33.8). That is more than enough to show why we must fear the Lord God. Go to the concordance and look up fear. It is a lot to count. However, the point here is we all need to fear the Lord.

When we sin, do we feel as they felt? Guilt or what? Sometimes, it is hard to show guilt and bring about a confession because o f fear of what would happen to you. We cannot possibly get away with it. But, then, when you don't feel guilty about it, even if you have done wrong, you better expect the unexpected from the Lord God. That's when the Lord God decides to do something about it. And when He does – fear will come upon you when you realize what you have done wrong. This is exactly what happened to Israel when God sent the fiery serpents upon them. The showed fear of God's wrath. The fear of the Lord is a different kind of fear than the first because He created you in His image, and you show more respect for Him in complete trust and obedience, seeking His will in your life.

What, then, is sin? 1 John 3.4 says that sin is lawlessness. Regardless – what does it mean? It means that without proper law (a set of rules and regulations) to guide us, we do things that are wrong even if we don't know it. Sin entered that perfect state of man in the Garden of Eden and has long been destroying mankind through the evil heart of Satan. Sin, therefore, is falling short of the glory of God (Romans 3.23). We are missing the mark. When you take up archery, you will practice with a good bow and arrow. The aim is to shoot the arrow where it is supposed to go, but then, at times, you would fall short of the aimed target. This is the same thing when we say we fall short of God's glory – His salvation. It is rebellion (not obeying), unbelief (not believing in the truth), and trespassing (putting your foot in the wrong place). 1 John 5.17 says that all unrighteousness is sin. Therefore, sin is a volitional act of disobedience against God's will. Sin is not spiritual, but it is paganism.

God hates sin because it is the very antithesis of His nature (Romans 1.18; Psalm 11.5; Proverbs 6.16-19; 15.9; Psalm 5.4-5; 7.11;). It opposes His very nature and is the work of the devil (John 8.44). Sin separates us from God (Isaiah 59.2). He does not like anything defiled in His holy domain. When God called Moses from the burning bush, He told Moses to take off his sandals because he was entering the holy ground. Sin was first noticed in Satan when he tried to exalt himself above the Lord God. He was the leader of a group of angels. He led this group of usurpers to the throne of glory. What Satan didn't understand was the fact that God had created him to be what God wanted Lucifer to be. Lucifer/Satan had too much pride and had gotten carried away and disobeyed the Creator and had deserved judgment for his careless behavior. The Lord God knew what was about to take place when He created the heavens and the earth. Who is trying to get even with the Lord God because he was kicked out of heaven for rebelling against God. In Ezekiel, it describes Satan's unrighteousness found in him. Satan was created in perfection till his unrighteousness was found in him (Isaiah 14.12-17; Ezekiel 28.12-28).

"We have spoken against God and you." This is a confession from the children of Israel. We have spoken against God first because He is the Creator and Redeemer. He is also the Providence of our needs. We have spoken against God first because He is holy. Then we have spoken against God secondly because the person (Moses) was the leader and a chosen vessel of the Lord God to serve to meet the need , to give the best possible guidance , and to lead the way. We have spoken against you (Moses) because that person (Moses) is only human and has some weaknesses, but that person had sound judgment. And because it is through that person (Moses), the effect comes to the Lord God first and back to that person (Moses) at the same time. Moses was the leader chosen by God to lead Israel. He had to endure the reproaches and deal with the rebellious of Israel.

When we do wrong, we must confess in order that our wrong can be corrected, whether it be against God or man or both and even the church (the body of believers) (1 John 1.9-10). When we confess, it must be with true repentance. What is repentance? Is it being sorry for yourself? No, it is an act of being sorry for what you do wrong, not only for yourself but against God. It means to turn yourselfff around and turn over a new leaf. It means a voluntary change of mind, heart, and will and not try to make the same mistake again. True repentance must work with faith, for they are coupled together. Repentance toward God and faith and toward Jesus Christ are inseparable and is essential for salvation. Faith without repentance will not work; neither is the other way around. The failure to exercise faith for every reason we should trust God, who would often deliver in our need, is a grievous sin for which we must whereby be punished. "Faith is the assurance of things hoped for, the conviction of things not seen." (Hebrews .11.1).

We must practice repentance anytime we do wrong to break our fellowship with the Father (1 John 1.9; Job. 42.1-6). The Holy Spirit causes the inward change through the Spirit's convicting power (John 16.7, 11).

Because of God's loving-kindness, repentance is the gift of God (Acts 5.31). 2 Corinthians 5.17 says that old things are passed away, beholding all things becoming new. In other words, this means to get rid of your mistakes in your guilty past and start over again as a new creature (creation) in Christ.

You must confess that you did not mean to do these things. Romans 10.9 says that if you confess with your mouth either the Lord Jesus and believe in your heart that God has raised him from the dead or all your wrongs or both, then you will be saved or have your life rededicated to the Lord Jesus Christ. Notice the verse says you must believe that Jesus was raised from the dead. Here, we must accept this fact because it is the foundation of our faith. The Bible says without the resurrection of Christ. God would be declared dead, and our faith would be in vain (1 Corinthians 15.12-19).

Acts 17.30 points out the importance of repentance. The verse says that God now commands "all men everywhere to repent." The lost must repent – even the backsliders! No one in particular! The Apostle Paul says in 2 Corinthians 7.9 " Now I (Paul) rejoice, not that you were made sorry, but that your sorrow led to repentance." John 3.16 says the lost are to repent/confess or die. The backslider is to repent or become disciplined (Hebrews 12.3-11).

One important part about repentance from Hebrews 6.4-6: The writer says that it is impossible to renew repentance. There has been much debate over these verses, and at times, the most difficult to understand is what was in the mind of the writer, even when he was inspired by the Lord God to write these verses trying to tell us something. What the writer of Hebrews was trying to say in connection with the word impossible is that the professed Christian didn't truly believe. He is that person who so sins will find it impossible to repent again. Being religious was not enough, so says the Apostle Paul (Romans 12.1-2). These verses do not in any way have anything to do with the backsliders, for they can repent, and their fellowship with the Lord can be restored. The Apostle Peter backslid, but he repented after he denied the Lord 3 times and was restored to the fellowship of the Lord (John 21.3-17). 1 John 1.9 is very clear to say that any Christian, whether faithful or backslider, can repent, and God is always ready to forgive, and fellowship with the Father can be restored.

Since being religious is not enough to save you, it is proof of this fact. They may have professed but did not possess eternal life. They may look like Christians from the outward appearance, but the Lord knows the heart of man that, from the inward part of him, did not truly repent. They must have genuine repentance to show proof that they are truly saved. We can cite one person from the Old Testament as an example of those who would find it impossible to renew. We can take Esau (Genesis 25.27-34). He sinned much against the Lord God when he sold his birthright to Jacob for a bowl of lentil stew.

Later, he tried to repent but found it impossible to do so, for the Bible says, "He found no place of repentance though he sought it diligently with tears." Esau, as an example, is an exact picture to bring to light these difficult verses. He gave up his birthright to Jacob because he said he hated his birthright, only to realise his mistake and try to repent – but he found it impossible.

The Hebrew writer goes on to say they have "fallen away." The Apostle Paul says the same thing in Galatians 5.4: "You have become estranged from Christ, whoever of you would be justified by law; you have fallen from grace (New King James Version)." Matthew 7.21-23 says: Not everyone who says to me, "Lord, Lord, will enter the kingdom of heaven, but only the one who does the will of my Father who is in heaven" (New International Version). It goes on to say that Christ at His throne will declare that He never knew you and to depart from Him. This is righteous judgment! We need to be careful how we interpret because if we say that if a saved person sins – he has just lost his salvation; he just fallen away from grace. This is a very misleading doctrine. It is not for us to judge over this matter. If it is true, it is impossible to become saved a second time. The only way to know them is by their fruits (Matthew 7.16; 12.33).

Would the Lord God have mercy on those who try to show genuine repentance? The Apostle Paul says from Romans 9.15: For he says to Moses, "I will have mercy on whom I will have mercy, and I will have compassion on whom I will have compassion" (also Ex.33.19). Is this the justice of God even when He is the God of love? We cannot question God's attributes. Romans 3.6 says, ' How would God judge the world then?' Then the Roman writer goes on to say that there is no one – none perfect in the eyes of the Lord God and that He is no respecter of persons (Romans 2.11; 3.10).

After the Israelites had confessed their wrong doing, they asked Moses to intercede with the Lord. Why? So that the Lord God would remove the serpents from them. To intercede is in the New American Standard Version, while in the King James Version, it means to pray. Moses was acting as a go-between (as mediator) and has been from the time God called Moses. Moses is the type of Christ who acted as a mediator between the sinner and God when He went to the cross to die for our sins and still is the mediator making intercession (prayer) with the Father for us (I Timothy 2.5; I John 2.1).

In Old Testament times, since the laws of God were established, only the high priest acted as a go-between Israel and God when making sacrifices for the sins of Israel. In this way, the high priest would have access to the Holiest of Holy of the Almighty Lord God to receive forgiveness. Now we have access to the Father through Jesus Christ our Lord (John 14.6).

There are three things about prayer we will need to look into: (1) What is prayer? (2) How do we pray? (3) What is the purpose of prayer and its effect? There are several questions pertaining to this matter, but these three are sufficient to give us the general meaning. I do not intend to be exhaustive on the subject – just enough to put the meaning through.

A.   What is Prayer?

It is like two people talking to each other during a coffee break about different things. It is talking to God as a means of communication with each other. It is like a son who wants to ask his father several things pertaining to life, school, homework, and such. We are like that, but we do not expect miracles from them because we are all humans and weak with limitations. We have to depend on the Heavenly Father for miracles because He created us to be what He wants us to be.

Matthew 7.7-8 is a prayer verse, and they give us an idea of what prayer is. It is an admonition of the concept of prayer. Prayer is as old as man. Prayer is practised in different ways. When we pray, we pour it out of our hearts with a need – something that can be beyond our control to meet. Prayer is man's acknowledgement of being higher than himself. These verses explain how or what we can do with prayer when we pray. It is talking to God, making our request known to Him in faith. It is asking and receiving, seeking to find. Once we find what we're looking for, knock, and the door will be opened to meet your needs. When we ask to receive, ask in humility. We must first seek the kingdom of God.

There is a difference in seeking his kingdom . We may refer to seeking out the Father's Will or the heart of the Father or both. When we seek out God, we must look for an open door, for there are many avenues for us to look to find. We would have to keep on knocking until the Father answers the knock. Don't expect a prompt answer. It requires time and patience. I Thessalonians 5.17 says to pray without ceasing. You are under God's testing when you pray as you seek out His will. This verse is saying don't give up – keep on going. It requires a mountain-moving faith until it perseveres the impossible. The Bible points out that nothing is impossible with God, for everything is possible through prayer (Luke 1.37; Mark 10.27; Jeremiah 32.17).

B.   How do we pray?

When we pray, we must first realize its reality. God does not want us to play games with Him. Get into your own subconscious self and just surrender completely to the Lord God when you become ready to submit yourself in to deep meditation. Everything we say as we pour them out of our hearts must be serious in nature. We do not beat around the bush. We need to get into the serious business of prayer. There are several ways we can pray.

We go to the Father in humility and in faith. That is the first important essential. Our prayers must be in earnest and not amiss anything without wavering (James 1.6; 4.3). We must be conscious of our reproach toward the Father, for He is holy so that we can have a close relationship (Psalm 69.19; 74.22; 119.22, 39; 1 Timothy 4.10; 1 Peter 4.14).

We should first thank God above all else and for the Lord Jesus Christ and what He has done for us. Then we pray for those around you – your family and friends, your church especially your pastor and his family, and those without Christ. Lastly, pray about yourself and your needs and other needs which may be of deep concern. The Apostle Paul says in Philippians 4.19:

"He will supply all our needs in accordance to His riches in glory by Christ Jesus." He continues to say we should not be anxious for nothing but in everything by prayer and supplication. We should let our requests become known to God (vs.6-7). This is an idea of prayer that should be prayed in this manner, and don't forget to pray in the name of Jesus Christ because there is a wonder-working power of Christ that worketh through all righteousness. It doesn't matter how you pray because it depends on the circumstances, but pray humbly. Even the demons fear the name of the Lord (James 2.9). Here in James 2.9 is in effect saying, "You say you believe in Jesus, you do well, the demons do too, but they tremble at His name in fear – do you? And the demons do believe, fear, tremble, and cry, saying, "Jesus, the Son of the Most High God."

We must be relaxed when we talk with the God the Father. Act normal, just as we do when talking with one another. We should show fear and respect before the Holiest of Holies. There should be no reason to be tense. Do not be afraid to ask. We are at ease! We would be able to pour out our hearts when we make the right approach. The Holy Spirit does that for us as He searches out our hearts and minds, working up our deep convictions. When we visit someone, the host usually makes us feel welcome and feel "at home" and not make us feel out of place. This is the idea of making yourself feel at home with the Father. Just be yourself and make yourself comfortable.

When we pray, we should not make repetitions – in other words, don't say the same thing over and over. It doesn't help to have our needs met. We can ask what we have in mind at different times. The Bible points out that God the Father knows our needs ahead of time before we ask, but it is important to ask regardless (Matthew 6.8).

C.   What is the purpose of prayer, and how does it affect us?

The question here is to say why do we pray and how does it help us. The purpose is numerous, and they can be of greater effect once we take up the practice. Prayer has proven to be very effective and influential. Prayer does change lives and has done the impossible. Through prayer, nothing is impossible with God (Matthew 19.26; Luke 1.37; Mark 10.27; Jeremiah 32.17, 27). Why pray is very obvious from the text verse: "So that God may remove the serpents from us (Numbers 21.6)."

The Israelites were overcome by the serpents because of their sinful behaviour against God and Moses. Once confessed, then forgiveness is granted. Genuine repentance must be the obvious (Ezra 10.1-44). What is genuine repentance? It involves heartfelt sorrow before God for our sins and prompt action to correct them. Repentance is not a mechanical duty but rather a heartfelt response to the conviction of sin. It involves not only grief over sin but also includes a decision to change one's ways. Therefore, prayer will get you out of all your troubles or the serpents in your life (Psalm 34.6). Prayer is renewal. It is the refreshing of your mind, heart and soul. It is the making of the whole self completely in God's own hands so that He can mould us the way He wants us to be. He is the potter, and we are the clay (Isaiah 64.8; 29.16; Jeremiah 18.3-4). If and when He sees any broken chips in our lives, He will remould us and make us new again. It is like a watch . God is rewinding our lives and starting the day right each day. He rewinds the springs of life in us whenever He meets our needs when we pray.

Why Pray? Because Luke 18.1 says that Jesus urged men to pray. When He told them a parable, He said, "They should always pray and not give up (NIV)." Prayer is the only way to get things from God (James 4.2). It is a channel of power and blessing (Jeremiah 33.3). Sinners can become saved through prayer (Romans 10.13-14). It is casting all your cares to the Father when your soul becomes troubled, and He will take care of you (1 Peter 5.7).

There are some hindrances to prayer we will need to consider (1 Peter 3.7). What does it mean when we hinder? It means to hold back , put off , or something lacking. It is like holding back a secret that will hound us for a long period of time. There are several reasons, depending on the circumstance from which you may not have received an answer from the Lord God. That is when you get into trouble for becoming chastised. Unbelief is one of the dangers in the life of the Christian (James 1.6-7; Hebrews 11.6).

Another danger is an unforgiving spirit (Matthew 5.22, 24). What this means is that you may have had something held back that needs to be corrected. If you had a grudge or if you had sinned against your Christian brother, then you must go to him for forgiveness before you go to the Father in prayer because if you don't, you would be in danger of God's anger over your behaviour. Your fellowship can be restored once the problem becomes corrected, or else the case would go before the church council or the church as a whole to have it straightened out before it gets ugly or out of control. This will prevent division within the church. The Apostle Paul had to deal with the divisions of the Corinthian church. Matthew 5.22-26 mentions about going to court. It depends on the seriousness of the case. However, depending on whatever the case may be, first square it away with your brother in Christ or else go before the church to help absolve the problem. Even though forgiveness is a choice, we have to make it time and time again. We need to be tolerant of one another. It is why God requires this of us, even though it is painful. I have the occasion of going through the same thing in the past. It was not easy, but it helps to alleviate the pain.

Now, the question comes to most of our minds. Will God the Father answer prayers? It has long been a very troublesome question that has perplexed many of us. The answer is God will answer depending on the outcome of the situation. John 15.7 says – "If you remain in Me, and My words remain in you ; you will ask whatever you desire, and it shall be done for you" (Modern English Version). The Bible says to abide in the Spirit who indwells in us (Ephesians 5.18; Rom.8.14), and the Spirit will carry out our requests.

Moses interceded for the children of Israel. Moses was a great leader and man of faith, having had to put up with the Israelites even though he had made some mistakes in his life. Moses was very reluctant to bear the responsibility as their leader. Therefore, we should be reluctant to carry out our own responsibility to pray about everything without ceasing (1 Thessalonians 5.17) by permitting the Holy Spirit to take control. Furthermore – don't copy the behaviour and customs of this world, but be a new and different person with a fresh newness in all you do and think (Romans 12.1-2; Ezekiel 18.30-31). Then, you will learn from your experience how the Father's ways will satisfy you.

From the study of Amos 5, we will learn from it a call to repentance, and the chapter explains how we can turn around from our ways and look up to the Lord God. Let us share a few verses from it. They are from the New International Version:

5.4 - "This is what the Lord says to the house of Israel: Seek Me and Live!"

5.14 – "Seek good, not evil, that you may live; then the Lord God Almighty will be with you, as you say he is."

5.24 – "But let justice roll on like a river, righteousness like a never-ending stream." Finally, "So is my word that goes out from my mouth: It will not return to me empty, but will accomplish what I desire and achieve the purpose for which I sent it (Isaiah 55,11)." So, what do we have in summarization?

1. Realize your wrongdoing.
2. Pray about it.
3. Confess it.
4. Forgiveness will be granted.
5. Then go your way.

Chapter 4:
The Brazen Serpent: You Are Delivered!! (Numbers 21.8-9)

The Lord said to Moses, "Make a snake and put it up on a pole; anyone who is bitten can look at it and live." So Moses made a bronze snake and put it up on a pole. Then, when anyone was bitten by a snake and looked at the bronze snake, he lived (New International Version).

LOOK AND LIVE!! This is the key to salvation. Here, this incident is one of the chosen prophecies by our Lord Jesus Christ from the Old Testament prophecies to illustrate his own person and work (John 3.14-15) and was fulfilled (Matthew 27.46). It is an interesting type of judgment/deliverance God had imposed on the children of Israel, later to become fulfilled on the cross of Christ.

First, from the preceding verses, we read of the divine judgment, and now we are looking at the divine deliverance. Here, the Lord God was displaying an act of love for the people of Israel. The Lord God also displayed His divine forgiveness.

When Moses interceded, God answered back with an instruction to make a fiery serpent and put it on a pole. Notice that the word fiery is left out of the NIV, whereas it is listed in the KJV and in most other translations.

Now, why did God say to make it fiery? The answer is obvious in verse 9. Moses made it out of bronze or brass. Note that God did not describe how the fiery snake is to be made out of. Moses already knew from experience the relation to the bronze altar from which it was symbolized as the type of divine judgment (Exodus 27.2). Self-judgment also occurred with the brass laver. The altar and the laver are part of the Tabernacle.

Numbers 21.8 signifies that the serpent was the type of sin that correlates to Jesus Christ, who accepted the sin of the world. Verse 9 signifies that the brass or bronze was the type of judgment that correlates to the cross of Calvary. Therefore, the brass serpent was a picture of sin punished and judged. The idea also applies to Jesus Christ on the cross when we look up to it having our sins punished and judged. For the children of Israel, it was a necessity of personal faith for salvation.

The question: Why brass? It is generally rendered as bronze or copper. Brass – the yellow alloy of copper (85%) and zinc (15%) being golden or reddish in colour and has greater strength and ductility than copper, having an excellent resistance to corrosion. It is largely used as a modern material, while bronze (copper and tin) was used to a greater extent in ancient times. Bronze was the principal material through the ages for all manner of articles and ornaments. It was used daily.

Israel was having a very critical experience of God's wrath since leaving Egypt. Since God sent the fiery serpents as a form of punishment, there were no known antibiotics or serums like we have today to cure the poisonous bites. However, this case was of divine means, and the only cure was divine forgiveness. Everything that took place was directly from the Lord God. The indication here was a vital command on God's people to show faith in God's Word and trust in Him. They had only to believe that God would do what He promised to those who would look up to the lifted serpent. In reality, there was nothing magical about the serpent to give out the healing power. It was the glory of God surrounding the lifted serpent. All you had to do was look up, and you will feel the glory of God surrounding you with forgiveness.

Verse 9 shows that there was an invitation of deliverance. The Lord God was inviting those who were bitten by the serpents to look up to the brazen serpent in order to live. There may have been those who showed unbelief and died. The Book of Hebrews displays the warning against unbelief and hardening of hearts (3.7-19). Read also 4.1-13. This is exactly the same picture with Jesus Christ when He went to the cross. God the Father, furthermore, extended that precious moment of invitation to those who would look up to Jesus Christ and never die but have everlasting life (Jn.3.16). It is also a divine deliverance to anyone who would look up to the cross.

It is a test of faith to look and live, and this is fulfilled in Romans 8.3-4 and 2 Corinthians 5.21. In Romans, it plainly says that the law was weak through the flesh, that it could do nothing to save us from our wrongdoing, nor could it forgive us and make us justified. It was obvious the law was spiritual because the law was given by God. However, the flesh became carnal and was unable to grasp the spirituality of the law because the flesh was sold under sin – bound to it from the beginning (Romans 7.14). Romans 7.7-25 is an interesting passage explaining the nature of carnality fighting with the true concept of spirituality, at the same time trying to live with the law but instead finding that the carnal self was bound under the law and was not able to cope with life's problems. The carnal self was trying to do what was right. The carnal self had quite a struggle until Jesus Christ came along, who knew no sin to become sin for us (2 Corinthians 5.21).

Therefore – the question: When the test of faith is shown in this verse during the time of God's invitation, then what is faith? Hebrews 11.1 says: "Now faith is the assurance of things hoped for, the conviction of things not seen." The key is not seen. It is the only definition found in the Bible. In other words, it is saying with all the hope for the things of sustenance, we should accept the the things we have not personally seen without a doubt. It is accepting the proof of things not seen (2 Corinthians 4.18). If we are to believe in something, then that would be faith; however, we depend on faith to guide us in all truth and not be tossed about in different directions or doctrines (James 1.6). As long as the believer produces faith, he should keep his eyes fixed on Christ, not looking neither to the left nor the right (Hebrews 12.2). This verse also indicates that Christ Jesus is the author and finisher of our faith who, with the joy sought before him having had endured the cross, despising the shame, and is sitting at the right side of the throne of God right at the moment. So, the true meaning of the believer is to have assurance through trusting and obedience to accept the spiritual reality. It is the acceptance of the things unseen as proof. It is confidence in God. With faith, all things become possible. There are many ways we can do with faith, and there are all kinds of faith. Therefore, we cannot do anything without faith.

After the believer has had his eyes upon Jesus and not turning back, he has to place all of himself at the altar – at the foot of the crimson-stained cross (Romans 12.1) and be able to deny self (Hebrews 12.1; Luke 23.42). In Romans 12, we must present our bodies as a living sacrifice. We must be holy and acceptable unto God. This is the most reasonable – the most desirable way. Then Hebrews 12.1 shows a very interesting admonition to become aware of those surrounding us – watching us in all that we do that might display bad influence. Let us lay aside every weight and sin that besets us. Whatever hinders us from being the winner of the race (Philippians 3.12-14), from which we were encouraged to run with patience. The sin that beset us refers perhaps to unbelief/doubts. Then, we go on to try by faith to avoid any obstacles that would prevent our spiritual progress.

Faith can be displayed by all kinds of people depending on how they exercise it, whether it be big or small, in comparison to the mustard seed (Matthew 13.31). So, how does faith work affect us to some certain degree within our own spiritual environment? Faith could also mean forsaking all ; I take Him. This is exactly how faith works. Let us break this down. Forsake means to "forget about it" or "leave it behind." All means just about everything surrounding you, depending on whatever it is. Take means to accept or reject. He would be Jesus. It is trusting and believing without a doubt. So you have the picture – you would forsake all, turn around and not go back to the old ways and turn over a new leaf (2 Corinthians 5,17). Deny yourself! You cannot know your inner peace unless you have Christ in your life. Therefore, forsake everything and look up to Jesus and accept Him or take Him to be your Lord and Savior of your life.

When we look up at the cross where it has become stained with the blood of Christ , we will become purified. The Israelites looked up to the bronze serpent hung on the pole ; they became "purified" from the poisoned serpents God sent as a form of punishment for defying the Lord God. We became purified from sin when we looked up to Jesus. The issue here is purification from sin. Thus, begs the question: What is purification from sin? It means to become cleansed from sin. The idea was that when we became dirty, we would wash ourselves or take a shower, and we would use soap to become clean. It is the same way when the blood of Christ cleanses us from all unrighteousness (I John 1.9). In Biblical times, during Jesus' ministry, he healed certain people, and each time, he would tell them to go to the temple or a certain place for purification. 1 Corinthians 3.16-17 says we are the temple of God, and the Holy Spirit lives within us. Then it goes on to say that if anyone defiles the temple of God – God will destroy him. It also emphasizes that the temple of God is holy because God is holy.

In summarization, we have the following:

1. The Brazen Serpent
2. The Divine Judgment
3. Look and Live!
4. Purification of Sin

Chapter 5:

The Well: The Holy Spirit (Numbers 21.16)

And from there, they continued to Beer, that is the well of which the Lord said to Moses, "Gather the people together, so that I may give them water."

We will need to back up to verse 10 prior to the well. It was after the serpent incident they began to move on toward Moab. Here they are wandering again, but this time, it was the Lord's instruction for Moses to go to a certain place He had shown him and to have the children of Israel assemble there so that the Lord would give them water. It took a while for them to finally arrive at Beer. Beer is probably translated as well. We probably should not confuse Beer for a town in Judah to which Jotham fled for fear of Abimelech (Judges 9.21). This Beer is located somewhere near the border of Moab in the wilderness. Either the well was already there, or the children of Israel dug it up to receive the miraculous supply of water, which will be explained in the next chapter ; we do not know, but verse 18 indicates otherwise. All this will be explained further in Chapter 6. However, the narrative indicates they went there to receive some water from the Lord.

It is common knowledge that through the years, Israel had experienced a lack of water because the wilderness they had journeyed around was very dry and was mostly desert. They had grumbled a great deal through their ordeal. They had to depend on the Lord to provide provision to satisfy their physical need. The problem here is that they were never satisfied until that day.

It is interesting that through the wilderness experience, the Lord God was testing their faith and trust in Him. We can interpret this verse in several ways to receive some enlightenment of its application to us. We cannot take this out of context in a certain way as to how this will apply to us. We need to take a step back and make the connection.

Verse 16 would refer to the Holy Spirit, for it is a symbolic picture of having received the Spirit after looking up to Jesus as Lord and Savior. We are not talking about the baptism of the Spirit, for that is a very misleading doctrine. We are talking about being filled with the Spirit (Ephesians 5.18). It is like having received a whole new life all over again through the Spirit. The water here is speaking of the power of the Spirit to fill the believer to overflow with new spiritual life. It is also symbolic of Christ describing Himself as the Living Water when He met the Samaritan woman at the well (John 4.10, 13-14).

We become a partaker of the divine nature of the Holy Spirit. Jesus Christ comes to live in us in the power of the Holy Spirit. Romans 8.9 says:

"You, however, are not in the flesh but in the Spirit, if in fact the Spirit of God dwells in you. Anyone who does not have the Spirit of Christ does not belong to him." It is also described in John 7.37-39: On the last day of the feast, the great day, Jesus stood up and cried out, "If anyone thirsts, let him come to me and drink. Whoever believes in me, as the Scripture has said, 'Out of his heart will flow rivers of living water.' "Now this he said about the Spirit, whom those who. Believed in him were to receive, for as yet the Spirit had not been given, because Jesus was not yet glorified (English Standard Version). Here, it means Jesus has not yet gone up to the Father until after His resurrection.

The doctrine of the Holy Spirit is the most misunderstood when we misinterpret or misappell the Holy Spirit. The Holy Spirit has become a controversial issue among ourselves. We will need to grasp the doctrinal truth of the Holy Spirit. We must first understand the Deity of the Holy Spirit. The Spirit is God and is equal to God the Father and the Son Jesus Christ. The Spirit is not an "It", and we should not refer to Him as "It." The Spirit is a person, just as God and Jesus. Not only is the Spirit equal to the Father and the Son, but He is also eternal and existent.

They coexist from the beginning (Genesis 1.1,26; John1.1). Like God and Son, He possesses the attributes. The word Trinity is not in the Bible, but the idea is they all are equal as three in one.

The Christian doctrine of the Trinity comes from Latin, meaning threefold. It is a term used to denote the Christian doctrine that the Godhead exists as one God in three persons: Father, Son, and Holy Spirit. The Trinity is described as a group of three people or things as one. For example: "The wine was the first of a trinity of three excellent vintages." Another example is the state of being three: "God is said to be trinity in unity." We can use science and many other subjects to compare them as three in one. Like the Trinity, the number three denotes completeness. Let's take a look at a few other examples to prove the Trinity. The number 3 denotes completeness. The triangle has three dimensions to make a solid, which is one example. Some other examples are shown here:

1. Genesis 1.1 says that God, in the beginning, created the heavens and earth. First, we can look at our surroundings or, in our English language, described as the universe. We have space showing the three heavens . The first heaven is the atmosphere from where we live and breathe. Genesis 1.6-8 describes the expanse as Heaven. Then there is the second heaven, which is the outer space. This is where all the other planets are located, especially the Milky Way. Finally, the third heaven is outside the realm of the second heaven. This is God's realm. We do not know where it is because it is unseen. It is said that when Jesus returns, the heavens will open. This is where Jesus comes from – God's heavenly realm. Thereby describes three parts of heaven as described in Genesis 1.

2. In 2 Corinthians 12.2-4, the Apostle Paul describes that he knew a man having been caught up to the third heaven described as paradise (v.3). He also, in verse 4, says that what he heard could not be described in his writings. I would surmise that what he has seen in heaven, he was told not to describe anything that he has seen.

3. The universe is made of three elements: time, space, and matter.

4. There are three divisions to express time: past, present and future.

5. Space has three dimensions: length, breadth and depth.

6. Matter is made of three forms: solid, gas and liquid.

7. Three kingdoms are comprised of animals, vegetation and minerals.

8. Three persons in grammar to express and include all of mankind's relationships.

9. Man is created in God's image: body, mind and soul (1 Thessalonians 5.17). Therefore, he is one person. I Thessalonians 5.23 shows that we have 3 in 1 in ourselves being our "whole spirit and soul and body be kept blameless at the coming of our Lord Jesus Christ."

10. Then we have what is called time, and it comes 3 in 1 being that we have the past, the present and the future.

11. Note also in Matthew 28.19 where Jesus instructs the apostles: "Go therefore and make disciples of all nations, baptizing them in the name of the Father and of the Son and of the Holy Spirit." Here, Jesus names all three in one, denoting by saying "and of."

One last thing about the meaning of three as being complete. Jesus describes himself as being "three in one" in John 14.6. John 14.1-6 talks about a place in heaven. Mind you, verse 6 cannot be taken out of context because it relates to the passage from verses 1-5. Let us take a look at verse 6. Jesus said: 1. I am the Way, 2. I am the Truth, 3. I am the Life. So He is saying, "I am the Way, the Truth, and the Life. He is all of that. But there is a connection here: NO ONE can go to the Father EXCEPT by Me. There is no other around to the Father unless you come to know Jesus as Lord and Savior first. Then, you can have access to the Father. We have heard this expression many times: "Not over my dead body" or "You have to come through me first." Therefore, this is the idea with Jesus. Take a look back to Numbers 21.7. What happened here? The people of Israel had to go to Moses with a confession. Then Moses prayed to the Lord. So you see, what had to be done must go to the source first because they couldn't bypass Moses. We have to go through Jesus first before we have access to the Father. It is the same way with the high priest when submitting a sacrifice for the people of Israel whenever they sinned; then the high priest will enter the Holy of Holies to have access to God the Father. Now, with Jesus, all that has changed.

The Holy Spirit also possesses the divine attributes that the Father and the Son have:

1. He is everywhere present in the universe (Psalm 139.7-10).
2. He is all-powerful (Luke 1.35).
3. He is all-knowing (1 Corinthians 2.10-11).
4. He is eternal (Hebrews 9.14).

The Holy Spirit is in the presence of the lives of the believers at this moment. He is at work while Jesus is sitting at the right hand of the Father, making intercession for us (Romans 8.34; Acts 7.55-56; Ephesians 1.20; Colossians 3.1; Hebrews 10.12; 12.2; 1 Peter 3.22; John 16.5-15). Jesus describes the work of the Holy Spirit while He is away to be with the Father in heaven.

I will not attempt to write too much more about the Holy Spirit as it will require an exhaustive volume on the doctrine of the Holy Spirit. I will give some highlights of some of the things the Holy Spirit would do:

1. Convicts men of the sin of unbelief (John 16.9).
2. Convicts men that Jesus is the righteousness of God (John 16.10 – also Romans 10.34).
3. Regenerates the believer (John 3.5).

4. Indwells the believer (Romans 8.9-11; 1 Corinthians 6.19-20).
5. Seals the believer (Ephesians 1.13-14).
6. Infills the believer with power ((Ephesians 5.18; Acts 1.8).
7. Leads the believer to all truth and administers the spiritual gifts (1 Corinthians 12.1-11).

The Holy Spirit came to do the work of the church and will continue doing so until the work is completed to the coming of Christ at the Rapture.

The water given to the Israelites also signifies the Lord as the Living Water (John 4.7-15) . What this means is that through Him, we become channels of blessings to others who need Christ in their lives, sharing with them the glorious power of the gospel. It also means the new birth through the Spirit (John 4.1-8). We all have experienced the new birth or born again in Christ. When Jesus offered the living water to the woman at the well, He was offering her a chance of a new life in God through Him because she was an admitted sinner. She made a confession (John 4.16-18).

It was obvious the children of Israel misunderstood God's loving care for them because they failed to understand the enlightenment of His miracles. It is the same way in which we may have misunderstood the enlightenment of Jesus Christ our Lord, who died as a propitiation for our sins on the cross (Romans 3.25; 1 John 2.2; 4.10; 1.9; 2 Corinthians 5.21; Hebrews 9.14; Titus 3.5-7). In reality, the word propitiation means Christ's sacrifice for our sins on the cross. Christ's death on the cross satisfied God's wrath because it was prophesied, and it was all part of God's plan.

Having received the living water, it was through God's mercy He saved us – not by works of righteousness which we have done (Titus 3.5). Paul, in his writing to Titus, goes on to say it was done by the washing of regeneration and receiving of the Holy Spirit. God the Father poured on us the Holy Spirit through Christ that having been justified by His grace, we should become heirs according to the hope of eternal life (Titus 3.6-7).

Receiving the living water is partaking of the divine nature of God. By that, you can avoid God's chastisement if you go wrong only if you can trust and obey and believe in His miracles. It is the righteousness of God who has made you to become quicken in the Spirit (1 Peter 3.18; Romans 8.11; Ephesians 2.1; Psalm 119.107). To be quicken means to make alive, give life or vitality; to give life and to preserve life and to be made alive. Quicken us to walk in the Spirit! You must be filled with the Spirit at all times so that you will not stumble. To be filled in to be possessed by the Spirit who empowers you through the leading and controlling of your life (2 Corinthians 12.9; Acts 1.8; 2 Peter 1.3-4; Philippians 4.13). In this way, you would have an abundant life – a life complete in Christ. In other words, living the Christ-like life by following His footsteps (1 Peter 3.21).

And when Israel dug up the well, they sang this song of joy. It was a joy to have received some water. It was a joyful satisfaction. It is very common for Israel to sing such songs depending on the circumstances, whether it be for joy or for victory or whatever it may be. Joy comes in different concepts. It can come on account of a good conscience. It would mean happiness, praise, and thanksgiving (2 Chronicles 5.13; 2 Corinthians 4.15, 9.11; Jeremiah 30.19; Nehemiah 12.46-47; Psalm 9.1; Philippians 4.6-7; Colossians 3.16-17; Psalm 95;2-3). There are many more verses, but these are more than sufficient. It also means to become very elated with delight. Psalm 32.11 says: "Be glad in the Lord, and rejoice, O righteous, and shout for joy, all you upright in heart!" I Peter 1.8 says that by faith, you should have all joy upon believing in Him, having not seen Him. You should rejoice with the unspeakable joy and to be full of glory. When we have joy, it renews our strength or our spirit, and when we do, we show respect for the Lord God, serving Him with fear and rejoice with awe and reverence (Psalm 2.11).

While we seek the Lord God with gladness, we would love His salvation and continue to magnify (to broaden) His Name with rejoicing (Psalm 40.16). Isaiah 12.1-5 is the psalms of praise for God's deliverance. We are exactly like these verses shown. Let us take a look at it:

Verse 1 shows the prediction of that certain day when we would proclaim praise to the Lord God because before that day, the Lord God poured His anger on us whenever we do wrong. Then, when we pleaded to the Lord God in prayer, confessing our wrong, He turned away His anger and began to comfort us – showed His love and grace with divine forgiveness.

Verse 2 declares our beholding the salvation of the Lord. We should not be afraid when we put our trust in Him. We would declare His strength and song to our soul, having become our great salvation.

Verse 3 brings out our joy displayed over the asters drawn from all the wells of salvation.

Here, this verse shows the exact picture of the children of Israel during their times and trials in the wilderness. They sang with joy over the wells of salvation when they drew water from them. So, as we seek out the Lord, we would ask. Him to quench the thirst of our soul.

Verse 4 says on a certain day, we will proclaim the Lord with praise. We will call upon His name and share with the world what He has done for us, making mention of the exaltation or how great is the name of the Lord.

Then, finally, we will sing praise, declaring all the excellent things He has done and that it is known throughout the world (v.5).

Sadness can turn to joy whenever you make a petition to the Lord, and when God answers your prayer, you will rejoice. We will take Hannah, for example, in I Samuel. Chapters 1 and 2 tell us the story of Hannah's sadness of heart (1.8). Verse 1 reveals her distress, and she prayed to the

Lord God regarding her barrenness. She had finally bored a child and that the child would be given over to the Lord for dedicated service to Israel. It was granted.

As the story goes – She later became conceived, and in due time, after the Lord's remembrance, she gave birth to Samuel. Chapter 2 reveals her praise of thanksgiving to the Lord because she was satisfied and rejoiced. It is through her faith she trusted in the Lord God and was obedient to God. It was a song of praise and thanksgiving. She sang this song to pour out her joyful thanks unto the Lord God. It was in response to God's answer to her prayer. Her confidence was displayed toward the sovereignty of the Lord. She goes on to praise God's holiness (2.2), His foreknowledge (2.3), His power (2.4-8), and His judgment (2.9-10). This is to show that God is the God of love and was able to grant Hannah's petition by His divine providence.

Unlike Hannah, some of us have failed to grasp God's love and His providence. The children of Israel failed to see the light of God's miracles and their purpose. However, when judgment or chastisement befall on you because we made Him angry. Then, we come to realize our mistakes and go to the Father for His forgiveness. Your joy becomes full when He answers your needs. We must put complete trust in God's providence regardless of circumstances. When we err, we will suffer the consequences. Israel experienced this throughout the years of their wanderings since leaving Egypt and prior to enter ing the Promised Land. The Lord God sends us suffering and loss as a means of His chastisement. Our faith and trust in Him were being tested. However, we still rejoice in Christ Jesus. Habakkuk has shown this through his experience, and regardless, he still rejoiced in his God. He has made a very strong affirmation of this in Habakkuk 3.17-18. In all of this, the Apostle Paul says to rejoice always and ever under all kinds of circumstances, including suffering (Philippians 4.4; I Thessalonians 5.16). Paul had a thorn in the flesh that God put there, and he had suffered from it. He asked God to remove it, but God said His grace was sufficient for him and that His power was made perfect in weakness. Regardless, from the remaining verses of the passage (vs.8-10), he still counted as joy because when he was weak, he became strong. Note with interest the number three mentioned in verse 8 and again in verse 14. A coincidence? This is what I have been referring to previously: the completeness of the number three.

Ephesians 5.18-19 says that all believers are sealed with the Holy Spirit (Ephesians 1.13) when they believe – but not all are filled. It depends on their yielding to God's will (5.17). When you are sealed through believing in the Lord Jesus Christ by the Holy Spirit, you will be filled with joy , have courage , and seek spirituality by seeking out His Will for your life. In this way, you should be able to build up your Christian character.

Therefore, as you continue in your spiritual growth during your spiritual journey, struggling along, your soul shall be joyful in the Lord: It shall rejoice in his salvation (Psalm 35.9). In conclusion: "The LORD is my strength and my shield; in him my heart trusts, and I am helped; my heart exults, and with my song, I give my thanks to him" (Psalm .28.7.)

In summarization:

1. The Well
2. The Holy Spirit
3. The Trinity
4. The Living Water
5. Singing with Joy
6. The Life of Hannah

Chapter 6:
You Have Joy!! (Numbers 21.17-18)

Then Israel sang this song,

"Spring up, O well! Sing about it!"

The well the princes dug,

That the nobles of the people sank

with their sceptres and their staffs."

From the wilderness, they went on to Mattanah (Tree of Life Version, 2015). Verses 16-20 summarize Israel's journeys through the territory on the eastern side of the Dead Sea. They were celebrating the abundant well where the Lord had instructed Moses to go to this certain place (v.16).

The Israelites were elated with joy over the well the Lord had provided water to quench their thirst. As previously explained, water is symbolic of the Holy Spirit; hence, Christ described Himself as the Living Water (John 4.10, 13-14). It is the new life through the Spirit. Water speaks of His power to fill the believer to overflow with the spiritual life. We became the partakers of the divine nature – the Holy Spirit. Jesus Christ comes to live in us in the power of His Holy Spirit. Romans 8.9 says: "Now if any man has not the Spirit of Christ, he is not of His." Therefore, the Holy Spirit is the Holy Spirit of Christ. Christ Himself is the power of the Holy Spirit.

Now, we come to the point of Israel's joy over water. The word joy is the focus of this lesson. What is joy? Merriam-Webster describes joy as a feeling of pleasure or happiness that comes from success, good fortune, or a sense of well-being. It is something that gives pleasure and happiness. It is part of your emotion as a state of great delight or happiness. It is a giving of great pleasure , the expression or displaying glad feeling. This is what the Israelites were experiencing. They were filled with glad feelings – swelled with happy emotion.

Joy comes in different ways in life, whether it be from overcoming something, in marriage, in the home, or from church etc. Wherever joy is displayed, it shows a form of elation in a person or in some people together. Psalm 32.11 says: "Be glad in the Lord, and rejoice, O righteous, and shout for joy, all you upright in heart!" There are numerous verses in the scripture about joy. It is an account of a good conscience. It is happiness, praise and thanksgiving. It is being happy over something good. The Bible says laughter is good medicine for the soul. Proverbs 17.22 says: "A cheerful heart is a good medicine" (New International Version). But it also says a crushed spirit dries up the bones. You do not want to feel down or depressed. That was the way the Israelites went through. You need to have a cheerful heart. To be happy about something. The Israelites became overjoyed for a much-needed thirst to satisfy their souls. As I have mentioned , joy comes in different forms and attitudes. We can rejoice in His strength and salvation. Nehemiah 8.10 tells us that the joy of the Lord is our strength. When we have joy, it renews our strength. Nehemiah 8 and 9 tell us of the revival of Israel after their captivity. They were celebrating their freedom. Nehemiah says in 8.10 to go and celebrate with a feast. He encouraged them not to be dejected and sad – in other words, depressed. Why? Because through joy, the strength of the Lord was in them.

Psalm 2.11: "Serve the Lord with reverent fear, and rejoice with trembling" (New Living Translation). We show fear for the Almighty, for He is Holy.

Psalm 28.11: "The Lord is my strength, my shield from every danger, I trust in Him with all my heart. He helps me, and my heart is filled with joy. I burst out in songs of thanksgiving."

(New Living Translation). Here, the key words in this verse are trust, help and thanksgiving. All this is filled with joy.

Psalm 40.16: We magnify His name with joy. As we seek God with gladness, we would love His salvation and continue to magnify His name with rejoicing. The key word in this verse is salvation. Psalm 51.12 says: "Restore to me the joy of your salvation, and uphold me with a willing spirit (ESV)."

There is a song we used to sing, probably in camps or VBS: "I've Got That Joy." It goes like this:

I've got that joy, joy, joy down in my heart

Down in my heart, Down in my heart

I've got that joy, joy, joy, down in my heart

Down in my heart to stay.

And I'm so happy, so very happy ; I have the love of Jesus in my heart

And I'm so happy, so very happy . I have the love of Jesus in my heart

I have the love of Jesus, love of Jesus down in my heart

Down in my heart, Down in my heart

I have the love of Jesus, love of Jesus down in my heart

Down in my heart to stay.

You probably know the rest of the song, but it was a song of joy down in our hearts. We can sing a joyful song, as did the Israelites. It was a great joy in our lives when we took Jesus into our hearts and lives. That was joyful salvation.

We will remember the joy that Hannah displayed giving thanks to the Lord for His provision during her barren years. It was a lesson of faith in trusting in God's providence regardless of circumstances. She declared that even if God should send suffering and loss, she would still rejoice in the Savior God. It was one of the strongest affirmations of faith in all the scriptures.

Joy has a lot to do with the Christian life, as is shown in the Book of Philippians. This book will teach us the Biblical concept of joy. The life of the Christian is not possible without Christ. The Apostle Paul describes the Philippians as his joy and crown, encouraging them to stand firm in the Lord (4.1). Paul says in the book that we should be confident, which is the strength of promise. When. You have joy, love abound (1.9). Having joy in your Christian life will show great purpose in magnifying the Lord so that men might see Christ in you and be saved by Him (1.21-24). There is that privilege of salvation and suffering through joy (1.27-30). Therefore, let the joy of Christ become obvious in every area of life. Paul says in 1.21: "For to me, to live is Messiah and to die is gain" (Tree of Life Version 2015).

In summarization, we have the following:

1. Singing with joy.
2. Rejoicing in strength and salvation.
3. Magnifying His name with joy.
4. Joy in the life of a Christian

Chapter 7:

You Have Power and Victory! (Numbers 21.21-35)

"Awesome God from his sanctuary; the God of Israel – he is the one who gives power and strength to his people. Blessed be God!" (Psalm 68.35).

"He gives power to the faint, and to I'm who has no might he increases strength" (Isaiah 40.29).

"But they who wait on the Lord shall renew their strength; they shall mount up with wings like eagles; they shall run and not be weary; they shall walk and not faint" (Isaiah 40.31).

We will talk about power first, then victory, because they go hand in hand. First, we will take Psalm 68.35. We find the awesomeness and the greatness and the power and the glory and the victory of God from His sanctuary because as we enter the Holy of Holies, there is the awesome power of God being felt by the high priest who is the only sole person to enter the Holy of Holies. The psalmist says that God is the one who gives power to those who are weak and that those weaknesses gain strength from Him. He is to be blessed! He reflects His cosmic power. We recognize His awesome majesty because He is a Holy God and to be revered. It is foolish to depend on human strength instead of waiting for Him (Isaiah 40.29). Even though we may be strongest but get tired at times, God's power and strength never diminish. He is never tired or too busy to help and listen. His strength is our source of strength. When we feel all of life being crushed one way or the other, we cannot go another step. So remember that we can call upon the Lord God to renew our strength (Psalm 40.31). There is power in the name of the Lord. So, depend on Him to give you the power to overcome. Now, what does the power of the Lord God have to do to become victorious? Having power and becoming victorious come hand in hand. They work together.

Let us take a brief look at Numbers 21.21-35. Verses 21-35 tell of Israel's conquests between the two kings. In verses 21-32, the Israelites fought against Sihon, the king of the Amorites. The history is continued from verse 13. Chemosh was the god of the Moabites. Then, verses 33-35 illustrate the Israelites' victory over Og, the king of Bashan. Og was not an Amorite; however, he was designated as one (Deuteronomy1.18). According to Deuteronomy, the Israelites were forbidden by God to capture Moab and Ammon. There is a reason for this, as I will explain later.

First – We have a victory here three times (vs.1-2; 21-32; 33-35). However, they continued to have frequent failures and unfaithfulness to the Lord God with a show of courage and faith (v.34).

Secondly – Discouragement was shown often due to the severity and length of the journey of life. But it is a constant cause of sin.

Thirdly – The character of the serpents was shown:

        a.   Sin

        b.   Suffering

        c.   Sorrow

        d.   Supplication

        e.   Salvation (John 3.14; 2 Corinthians 5.21)

The story here was the look of faith, which was at once simple, searching (as a test), saving, and satisfactory.

According to Moses in Deuteronomy, he retells the story of the conquest of the land of King Sihon and how he was defeated (Deuteronomy 2.24-37). He gives several significant additions.

First, he shows that Israel's request to pass through Sihon's land was made in the best of terms (Numbers 21.21-22). It was a peace offering to the king. It was not an act of war, as Israel had offered to buy supplies. It was not Israel's plan to take the land but to pass through on the way to the Promised Land. But God had other plans. He had hardened Sihon's heart and thereby resisted Israel. He had done the same thing to the Pharoah before finally freeing Israel. This was God's first act in delivering the land over into the hands of the Israelites (Deuteronomy 2.30-31). Thereby defeating Sihon, the king of the Amorites.

Then, Deuteronomy 3.1-11 tells of the defeat of Og. Moses repents this account of the defeat (Numbers 21.33-35) with one significant addition. It was the Lord's hand any work (v.3). Verses 6-11 tell of the earlier account of this battle according to Numbers 21.33-35 by stressing the obedience and success of Israel taking the Transjordan as well as the kingdom of Og. As with the kingdom of Sihon, the whole kingdom of Og was destroyed.

The Transjordan is located east of the Jordan River. The Transjordan is now contained mostly in present-day Jordan. It was controlled by numerous powers throughout Biblical history, the Ammonites, Moabites and Edomites, who formed a strong chain of kingdoms until Israel's conquest. It was formerly a part of the land of Israel (Numbers 34.15), specifically the area allocated to the Israelite tribes of Rueben and Gad and half of the tribe of Manasseh.

There is much history of the present day of Israel prior to 1947 and 1948. In 1947, there was a background of the United Nations partition recommendation when the United Nations took up the question of Palestine, a territory that was then administered by the British. About 50 years before there was a movement called political Zionism that had begun in Europe. Then, in 1948, the state of Israel before then was called the Holy Land, being holy for all Abrahamic religions including Judaism, Christianity,

Islam and the Baha'i Faith. From 1920, the whole region was known as Palestine (under British Mandate) until the Israeli Declaration of Independence of 1948.

It was the Lord God's plan to drive out the nations and who gave ownership of the land. Deuteronomy 2.24-29 shows how the Lord God commands Israel to deal with other nations. It has to be the Lord God's way – not Israel. It was all according to God's plan when they engaged in battle. The Lord tells them what will occur His way. Deuteronomy 2.30 shows that the Lord God hardened the heart of Sihon so that He would not allow Israel to pass through his territory because God planned to deliver Sihon and his kingdom to Israel. It was the only explanation for giving this statement.

Deuteronomy was aimed at the new generation that had arisen during the wilderness journey because they were about to enter the Promised Land. They were encouraged to know the law and obey it. Deuteronomy consists of all of Israel's history first, from Sinai onward (Chapters 1-3). The second part of Chapters 4-26 is a review of important aspects of God's legislation for the people. Then, the third part of Deuteronomy is a preview of God's grace and government from Israel's entering into the land until the second advent of the Messiah (Chapters 27-33). Then, Chapter 34 closes with the death of Moses and the appointment of Joshua as the successor of Moses.

The point of Chapters 2 and 3 focuses on Israel's conquest against the kings of the Amorites and Bashan. The reason stated that the Israelites were forbidden by the Lord God to capture Moab and Ammon was that they had to wait upon God's time for them to capture the lands prior to entering the Promised Land. God did a very similar action against the Pharaoh by hardening his heart to let the people go. He did the same to Sihon and Og so that the Israelites could defeat both kings to capture the lands. This was after they sent spies to spy out the Promised Land. There were some giants occupying the Promised Land. Og was a giant. Here, hence, the real reason God did not want Israel to start their conquest. Deuteronomy 1.42-46 says: " But the Lord told me to tell you, 'Do not attack, for I am not with you. If you go ahead on your own, you will be crushed by your enemy. This is what I told you, but you would not listen. Instead, you again rebelled against the Lord's command and arrogantly went into the hill country to fight. But the Amorites who lived there came out against you like a swarm of bees. They chased and battered you all the way from Seir to Hormah. Then you returned and wept before the Lord, but he refused to listen. So you stayed there at Kadesh for a long time (New Living Translation). The Lord God had instructed Israel to wait on the Lord's timing to conquer the land, but Israel ran out of patience and could not wait. Isaiah 40.31 says, "Wait on the Lord." Also, Psalm 37.7: "Be still before the Lord and wait patiently for him; fret not yourself over the one who prospers in his way, not over the man who carries out evil devices."

Deuteronomy 2 gives us a little history of Israel's smashing defeat of Sihon the Amorite, king of Heshbon. Then, in Chapter 3, they secured Transjordan by defeating Og, king of Bashan, who had 60 fortified cities and many rural towns. All of this, the Lord God gave the land to Israel to live and settle. Everything done had to be according to the timing of the Lord God's leading, giving them victory. Those who entered the Promised Land were those who were twenty years old and under. Moses was unable to enter the land for his disobedience and would not let him cross the Jordan. However, he was able to view the Promised Land from the top of Mount Pisgah (verses 23-29).

Like wow!!! Here, it is a great application for us when we strive to live our Christian lives. Whenever we face many obstacles in our Christian walk, we do not try to overcome them by ourselves because we can be defeated if we do not know what we are doing to put up a fight. We have to depend on God's leading to help us to overcome our daily problems. I know this from experience. I have had some people – especially Christians – backstabbing me. I have had the occasion of confronting one person after calling for a meeting regarding the person's problem of backstabbing and poisoning my name. That didn't help. That person kept going, doing the same thing against me. Why was this happening? Because I did not pray to the Lord God asking for his help to do something about this person's continuing backstabbing and poisoning my name. To tell you the truth – that person was a Christian. She did not show her true colours as a Christian. I was not the only one who faced this problem from her. She has done the same against many others. You do not want to face God's wrath for destroying His work through His people who were trying to serve in the name of Jesus Christ. Regardless – I decided to just accept what this person has done and pray for her. I also prayed to the Lord to do what He needed to do to deal with her. I was at peace when she passed away from cancer.

1 Corinthians 3.10-4.5 , Romans 14.1-12, and 2 Corinthians 5.1-10 talk about the Judgment Seat of Christ. Only the Church Age saints or Christians will appear at that judgment according to 2 Corinthians 5.10: "For we must all appear before the judgment seat of Christ." The purpose of the bema (Greek for the judgment seat) is an exhaustive evaluation of our lives as Christians. 1 Corinthians 4.5 says the Lord will come and "bring to light the hidden things of darkness and reveal the counsels of the hearts. Then each one's praise will come from God." What this means is that God will not punish us as Christians and commit us to damnation (hell) but instead gives rewards to the victors. Each man's praise will come to him from God. He will not condemn us for our sins at that point because Romans 8.1 says, "There is therefore now no condemnation to those who are in Christ Jesus."

Therefore, what is actually the purpose of the judgment seat of Christ? It is to examine a Christian's total life. We will be recompensed for the deeds we have done, whether good or bad (2 Corinthians 5.10). It is the summing up and estimation of the total pattern of a believer's life. For example, our backbiting or destroying one's life by poisoning his/her name or whatever stupid stuff we have done during our Christian lives. This overall focus should keep us from worrying over every stupid action we have ever done. It is a time of reward, not punishment.

In summarization:

1. We have power and victory!
2. Overcoming obstacles
3. The Judgment Seat of Christ

Chapter 8:

Canaanland/Heavenbound!
(Deuteronomy 1.19-3.29 and Chapter 34

Let's recap: The life experiences of Israel's wanderings in the wilderness give us a great deal of life's everyday lessons and applications toward our Christian lives. We became examples of them. It is through our Lord Jesus Christ that we look up to the power of the cross that led us to become saved from sin. We fight life's battles as the Israelites did. We have to depend on God's leading through the power of the Holy Spirit. The Spirit guides us every step we go. He also teaches us all the ways of God's holiness and righteousness. Ephesians 4.23 says that we are renewed in the spirit of our minds and to put on the new selves created after the likeness of God in true righteousness and holiness. We can sing with joy and happiness. We need to bow on our knees before the Father that according to the riches of His glory, He may grant us to be strengthened with power through His Spirit in our inner being so that Christ may dwell in our hearts through faith (Ephesians 3.14-17).

Deuteronomy 1 tells us that in the 40th year, Moses spoke to Israel prior to entering Canaan, and the leaders of Israel were appointed. The Lord God instructed Moses to instruct Israel whom they would not enter the Promised Land and who would (Deuteronomy 1.34-40). It was the penalty for Israel's rebellion for not listening to Moses. Some of them were turned back to the wilderness and lived there since then. Those who entered the Promised Land later became a new nation. God took Moses to a high mountain to show him the Promised Land. This is what God said to him: And the Lord said to him, "This is the land of which I swore to Abraham, to Isaac, and to Jacob, 'I will give it to your offspring.' I have let you see it with your eyes, but you shall not go over there (Deuteronomy 34.4)." Moses was not allowed to enter the Promised Land. What the reason was is unknown. It could be his old age or he has done all he could leading Israel from Egypt to the wilderness for 40 years and it was time to turn over to new leadership to Joshua. He died in the land of Moab shortly after he was shown the Promised Land. It is believed that God buried Moses. It is unknown where he was buried. The death of Moses is recorded in Deuteronomy 34. Numbers 33 recounts the journeys of Israel, beginning with Egypt to Canaan. Then Deuteronomy 1.19-3.29 details the victory of Israel over Sihon, king of Heshbon and Og, king of Bashan. Then Deuteronomy 34 details the Israelites now in Canaan. The Lord God gives them instructions on the boundaries of the land of Canaan.

As the younger generation of Israelites entered Canaan – the Promised Land, they began their new lives in a new nation called Israel. We shall follow them there as well. It is called Heaven. Israel has experienced many footfalls through the years. The Lord God followed Israel through the years, from Saul to the last king of Israel. All that Israel had done was nothing new to the Lord God. It is the same with us as

Christians. It is through God the Holy Spirit who has been following us throughout our Christian lives in all that we do. We thank the Lord Jesus Christ for dying on the cross for our sins and arising on the third day in power so that we can become the first fruits of the resurrection (Romans 8.23; 1 Corinthians 15.20-28; 2 Thessalonians 2.13; Revelation 14.4). There is hope of the resurrection. Praise and glory be to God!!

Heaven bound! Heaven is a place of eternal bliss – eternal life. We read John 14.1-3: "Do not let your hearts be troubled. You believe in God; believe also in me. My Father's house has many rooms; if that were not so, would I have told you that I am going there to prepare a place for you? And if I go and prepare a place for you, I will come back and take you to be with me that you also may be where I am" (New International Version).

Revelation 21.1-3: Then I saw a new heaven and a new earth, for the first heaven and the first earth had passed away, and the sea was no more. And I saw the holy city, a new Jerusalem, coming down out of heaven from God, prepared as a bride adorned for her husband. And I heard a loud voice from the throne saying, "Behold, the dwelling place of God is with man. He will dwell with them, and they will be His people, and God himself will be with them as their God."

God has put eternity in our hearts and lives. Are you ready? We are Heavenbound! The Bible says that when we end our lives on earth, our bodies turn to dust again, and the spirit goes back to God who gave it

(Ecclesiastes 12.7). The spirit of every person who dies – whether righteous or wicked – returns to God at death. The spirit that returns to God at death is the breath of life.

(James 2.26; Job 27.3). It is obvious proof that there is no soul sleep here. Our souls go back to God while we sleep in the grave, awaiting His coming to take us up at the Rapture (1 Thessalonians 4.13-18). When Jesus comes to get us, we will rise and meet Him in the air. Our bodies from the grave will meet our souls in the air, and then we will be changed into glorious bodies. Hallelujah! Glory be to God! This is exciting. We will go to heaven when the roll is called up yonder! Unlike the experiences of new life in the new land of Canaan the Israelites went through, we will experience new life in heaven in our new glorious bodies because God will wipe away every tear from our eyes, and there will be no more death, sorrow, crying or pain. All things are gone forever (Revelation 21.4). No one in God's new kingdom will ever die. Death will cease at the destruction of Satan.

Israel continued to live in sin in the Promised Land. When we go to heaven, we will not live in sin any longer, as described above. The Promised Land was known as "The Land of Milk and Honey." It was first made to Abraham (Genesis 15.18-21) and to his son Isaac (Genesis 26.3), and then to Isaac's son Jacob (Genesis 28.13), and then finally to Abraham's grandson. It was supposedly from the River of Egypt to the Euphrates River (Exodus 23.31). But that had changed. Now, the new generation occupied

Canaan. What was left of the older generation not entering Canaan is believed to be the West Bank, called Palestine to this day. According to history, it is believed that the Palestinians claim partial descent from the Israelites and Maccabees, as well as all the other peoples who have lived in the region. The Land flowing with milk and honey, as described, heaven-bound, is described as a place of eternity with the Tree of Life at the center of it all. Revelation 22.2 says: "In the middle of its street, and on either side of the river, was the tree of life". Many researchers have wondered what happened to the Tree of Life when Adam and Eve were kicked out of the Garden of Eden. It is apparent that the Lord God took it out of the garden and placed it in the middle of its street in the place of eternity. The Tree of Life will yield fruit each month because the water flows from the sanctuary for food and the leaves for healing (Ezekiel 47.12).

For a more detailed description of Heaven, I would encourage you to pick up a book called "Heaven" by Randy Acorn. Are you ready to go Heavenbound?

Epilogue (Conclusion)

God's salvation is thus the springtime of the soul. There is a new quality of life at work within the human heart and the life of the believer. What is your life worth for this challenge? We find that God is disappointed in many lives. The aim of every life of a Christian should be to prepare for eternal life. Losing your life in the gospel means gaining a blessing from the Lord (Philippians 1.21). Living for Christ is not always easy and without trial. Others are the key to a Christian's life. Then satisfaction can be full and complete if we should "face up" to life and its environments. We will receive rewards (1 Corinthians 5.10).

Christianity is very challenging. The true value of life is in the spiritual realm, not in the physical ways of Satan (Romans 8.5-10). There are no limitations on whatever can be done by a life fully dedicated to Christ. We need to see the possibilities in our Christian living and deepen our sense of values. We need to open our lives for deeper inspiration and give our lives in service (Romans 12,1). I encourage you to seriously take the right steps in following Jesus Christ our Lord regardless of circumstances. The history of Israel from Egypt to the Promised Land is accounted as a very historical experience as they give us life's lessons to follow. Especially all the wars they went through. The Lord God guided them to victory. They have to depend on His guidance to guide them to victory. We became their examples of how we fight our life's spiritual battles. We have to depend on God's guidance in our lives and not become examples of the Israelites during their forty years of wandering in the wilderness.

May the grace and peace from God our Father and the Lord Jesus Christ be extended to you. Amen and Amen. Maranatha!

www.ingramcontent.com/pod-product-compliance
Lightning Source LLC
Chambersburg PA
CBHW060414090426
42734CB00011B/2308